Better Homes and Gardens®

⟶ 1990 ⟵
CHRISTMAS CRAFTS

ISSN: 1041-8016
ISBN: 0-696-01797-0

BETTER HOMES AND GARDENS® BOOKS

Editor: Gerald M. Knox
Art Director: Ernest Shelton
Managing Editor: David A. Kirchner
Project Editors: James D. Blume, Marsha Jahns
Project Managers: Liz Anderson,
    Jennifer Speer Ramundt, Angela K. Renkoski

Crafts Editor: Sara Jane Treinen
Senior Crafts Editors: Beverly Rivers, Patricia Wilens
Associate Crafts Editor: Nancy Reames

Associate Art Directors: Neoma Thomas,
    Linda Ford Vermie, Randall Yontz
Assistant Art Directors: Lynda Haupert,
    Harijs Priekulis, Tom Wegner
Graphic Designers: Mary Schlueter Bendgen,
    Michael Burns, Brenda Lesch
Art Production: Director, John Berg;
    Associate, Joe Heuer;
    Office Manager, Michaela Lester

President, Book Group: Jeramy Lanigan
Vice President, Retail Marketing: Jamie L. Martin
Vice President, Administrative Services: Rick Rundall

BETTER HOMES AND GARDENS® MAGAZINE
President, Magazine Group: James A. Autry
Editorial Director: Doris Eby

MEREDITH CORPORATION OFFICERS
Chairman of the Executive Committee: E. T. Meredith III
Chairman of the Board: Robert A. Burnett
President: Jack D. Rehm

1990 CHRISTMAS CRAFTS
Editor: Patricia Wilens
Contributing Editor: Liz Porter
Editorial Project Manager: Angela K. Renkoski
Graphic Designer: Lynda Haupert
Contributing Illustrator: Chris Neubauer
Electronic Text Processor: Paula Forest

Cover project: See page 60.

A roaring fire on the hearth, frost on the windowpanes, and snow in the trees summon visions of Christmases past, made dear by memories of handcrafted gifts and decorations. Make every Christmas merry with this treasure trove of holiday crafts. We've added many exciting new projects to our favorites from Better Homes and Gardens® *magazines.*

Join us for the pleasures of 1990 Christmas Crafts, a festival of holiday crafts that holds many possibilities for this year's gift-giving.

We hope these ideas and projects will be the stuff happy memories are made of for you and your loved ones for many Christmases to come.

Contents

Sugarplum Christmas

*Packages of dreamy treasures wait beneath
a beribboned pine decked in peppermint stripes
and sugarplum trims in this room full
of magic. Colorful candies and snuggly bears
promise sweet Christmas memories.*

A tree trimmed with ice-cream cones and gumdrop garlands starts off a candy-sweet Christmas with a family of furry Sugarplum Bears. Decked in their finest, Mama and Papa Bear, *right* and *opposite,* stand 32 to 33 inches tall, and Baby measures 30 inches—big enough for life-size bear hugs.

Simple sewing techniques turn a yard of fake fur, fabric scraps, and trims into lifelong pals for children.

Instructions for projects begin on page 12.

Candy treats spill over into every room in the house. In the dining room, *opposite,* starry moonbeam faces, candy canes, and a peppermint garland of braided rickrack adorn the tree. The men in the moon are made from smiling faces of painted modeling clay glued to cardboard stars.

Craft a candy-coated greeting, *right,* with assorted hard candies. Glued to a purchased form and coated with polyurethane, these colorful treats make a sugar-sweet wreath that lasts and lasts.

Festive cheer lingers through the winter in the candy-cane colors of ruffled 9-inch-square pillows with cross-stitched initials and the easy-to-sew Sugarplum quilt, *left.*

For the pillow, we've included a charted alphabet so you can stitch a personalized gift for family or friends on any even-weave fabric.

Scrap squares of red and pink fabrics make the quilt assembly perfect for either hand- or machine-piecing. Set on the diagonal, the Double Nine-Patch blocks are offset with plain blocks to make a quilt that measures 56½x66½ inches.

These project directions begin on page 15.

The story and music of "The Nutcracker" inspired these hand-crafted dolls, which are guaranteed to capture the heart of any dancing tot.

Our Toy Soldier Doll, *above left,* is the brave and romantic hero of the ballet's story and stands 26 inches tall. Purchased tassels, gold braid, and shiny buttons pro- vide the regalia for his high-stepping antics.

Scraps of shiny fabrics transform our muslin-body toy into a radiant Ballerina Doll, *above right.* This 24½-inch-tall flat-footed—and pigeon-toed—princess casts a winsome light on this musical drama. Dried flowers and purchased ribbon roses make a royal headpiece for her frizzy hemp hairdo.

Both dolls are easily made with simple mate-rials and techniques.

Plastic needlepoint canvas is the foundation for the 11½-inch-tall Gingerbread House, *opposite.* The house is worked in seven pieces with basic needlepoint stitches, then sewn together and embel-lished with lace and beads. The chimney "smoke" is a scrap of polyester filling.

Directions for these projects are on pages 18–23.

Gumdrop Garland

Shown on page 6.

MATERIALS
Gumdrops in various sizes
Monofilament
Large tapestry needle
Rubbing alcohol

INSTRUCTIONS
Note: To reduce stickiness, occasionally clean the needle and monofilament with alcohol as you work.

Thread the needle with monofilament cut to the desired length for the garland. String gumdrops from each end of the monofilament to the center, changing colors and sizes of the gumdrops randomly.

Knot monofilament around first and last gumdrops to secure ends.

Ice-Cream-Cone Ornaments

Shown on page 6.

MATERIALS
Sugar wafer ice-cream cones
2½-inch foam balls
Modeling paste
Acrylic paint in white and other
   ice-cream or sherbet colors
Paintbrush
Crafts glue
Polyurethane
Staples, hairpins, or paper clips
Scraps of pastel ribbons

INSTRUCTIONS
Apply six or seven coats of polyurethane to inside and outside of sugar cones. Dry thoroughly between coats.

Using crafts glue, glue a foam ball to each cone; let dry.

Spread a thin layer of modeling paste around the ball and slightly down onto the cone. Stand the cone in a drinking glass to dry. Remove any excess paste.

To create a holder for the hanger loop, insert a staple, hairpin, or bent paper clip into the center of the top of the ball. Swirl modeling paste over the ball as if you were frosting a cake, shaping as desired; let dry.

Mix acrylic paint with white to obtain pastel colors. Paint the ball; let dry. Cover the ball completely with polyurethane; let dry.

Insert ribbon or thread through the staple, hairpin, or paper clip. Tie ribbon into a loop to hang the ornament.

Sugarplum Bears

Shown on pages 6 and 7.
Finished bears are 30–33 inches tall.

MATERIALS
■ For all three bears
1½ yards of tan fake fur
¼ yard of tan corduroy for soles,
   face/muzzles, and lower jaws
Six ⅝-inch-diameter buttons for eyes
Scrap of light pink felt
Black pearl cotton
Scrap of lightweight cardboard
Polyester fiberfill
Carpet thread to match fur
Fabric glue
Stiff hairbrush

■ For clothing
⅜ yard of purple satin or moiré
   fabric for bib and bow tie
½ yard of green satin or moiré for
   vest, bib ruffle, and hat bow
⅜ yard of pink satin or moiré for
   straw hat
¾ yard of ⅛-inch-wide purple ribbon
   for bow tie
1 yard of ⅜-inch-wide pink ribbon
   for Baby Bear's bow
27x37-inch piece nylon net for veil
Small straw hat
1¼ yards of pregathered lace for
   collar
One ⅞-inch-diameter covered button
   for collar
¾ yard of ⅞-inch-wide green ribbon
   for vest ties
Four ½-inch-diameter covered
   buttons for Papa Bear's vest

INSTRUCTIONS
Note: Unless otherwise stated, ¼-inch seam allowances are included in the patterns; sew all pieces together with right sides facing.

Enlarge the patterns on pages 13 and 14 onto graph paper; mark and cut the patterns. Cut all the pieces, *except* tongues, from appropriate fabrics, reversing pieces when necessary and using the arrows on the patterns to determine the nap direction of the fur.

■ To make the bears
BODY: Sew front and back body pieces together along center front and center back seams.

Sew the legs together in pairs, leaving openings for turning and stuffing as indicated. On each leg, baste a sole to the foot bottom, matching dots to seams and easing to fit; sew in place. Turn legs right side out.

Lay the legs flat so center front and center back seams match; sew across top of each leg. Pin each leg to lower edge of body front, placing inside edge of each leg to either side of center front seam and having raw edges even. Sew legs to body along seam line.

Sew oval bottom to body bottom edge, matching dots to front and back body seams; sew through all layers, catching leg tops in the seam.

Sew the arms together in pairs, leaving openings for turning and stuffing as marked. Turn to right side; sew top edge of arms closed. Sew arms to body at sides, matching dots and having raw edges even.

Firmly stuff the body with polyester fiberfill through the top opening. Stuff the feet and legs through the side openings, leaving top inch of the legs unstuffed. Slip-stitch legs closed.

HEAD: Sew the head front to the head back, matching dots and easing the fabric around the curve; leave the bottom open. Stuff firmly.

Sew center front seam of muzzle. Stay-stitch around the remaining edge, ⅛ inch from edge. Stuff the end of the muzzle firmly; stuff the remainder less firmly. Set aside.

Sew the lower jaw from "a" to "b," leaving the back and top open. Turn; stay-stitch ⅛ inch from the raw edges.

Cut a tongue from cardboard. Use this as a pattern to cut a tongue from pink felt ¼ inch *larger* than the cardboard tongue. Lay cardboard on felt; fold felt edges over and glue to cardboard. Let dry thoroughly.

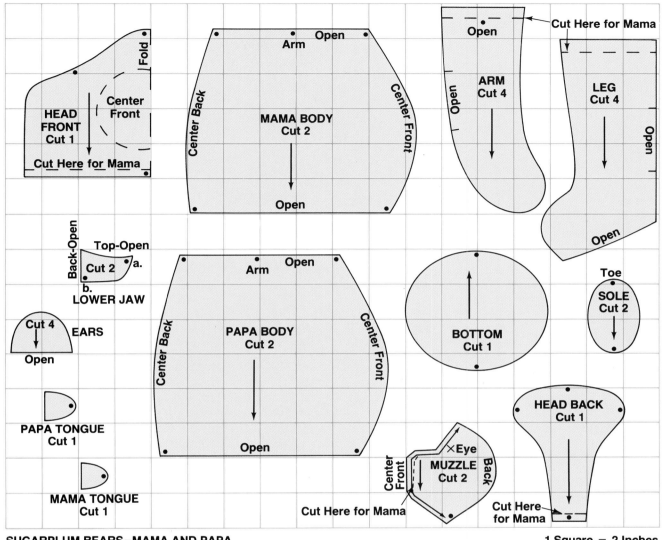

HEAD FRONT Cut 1

Center Front

Fold

Cut Here for Mama

Center Back

MAMA BODY Cut 2

Arm • Open

Center Front

Open

Open

ARM Cut 4

Cut Here for Mama

Open

LEG Cut 4

Open

Back-Open

Top-Open

Cut 2 a.

b.

LOWER JAW

Cut 4 **EARS**

Open

Center Back

PAPA BODY Cut 2

Arm Open

Center Front

Open

BOTTOM Cut 1

Toe

SOLE Cut 2

Open

PAPA TONGUE Cut 1

MAMA TONGUE Cut 1

Center Front

✕ Eye

MUZZLE Cut 2

Back

Cut Here for Mama

HEAD BACK Cut 1

Cut Here for Mama

SUGARPLUM BEARS—MAMA AND PAPA

1 Square = 2 Inches

Fold the top edge of the lower jaw to the inside along stitching. Slide the tongue into the lower jaw, matching the "a" on the lower jaw to the tongue dot; leave the back open. Whipstitch tongue and jaw together, sewing the felt edge of the tongue to the lower jaw edge.

Stuff the jaw through the back opening. Fold the opening fabric to inside; baste. Stuff firmly. Set aside.

Sew the ears together in pairs, leaving openings as indicated. Trim fur to shorter length on inside ear. Turn; whipstitch opening closed. Set aside.

ASSEMBLY: Turn the seam allowance on neck edge of head to inside. Pin the head to the body at the neck, matching the dot on the head back to the center back body seam and the center front of the head to the center front body seam. Using carpet thread, securely sew the head to the body.

Stuff the arms, leaving the top 2 inches unstuffed; slip-stitch opening.

Pin muzzle to head along dotted lines; sew in place, turning edge under along stitching. Using a double strand of pearl cotton, satin-stitch the nose

and straight-stitch a vertical line under the nose. See the photograph on page 7 for stitching details.

Align edge of jaw back to bottom edge of the muzzle. Sew securely across the bottom and the jaw back edge where it joins the muzzle. Run a narrow line of glue across the back of the tongue inside the mouth where it meets the muzzle.

Using carpet thread, sew the ears in place slightly in front of head seam. Sew on eye buttons. Brush the fur along the seam edges with a stiff brush to conceal the seams.

continued

13

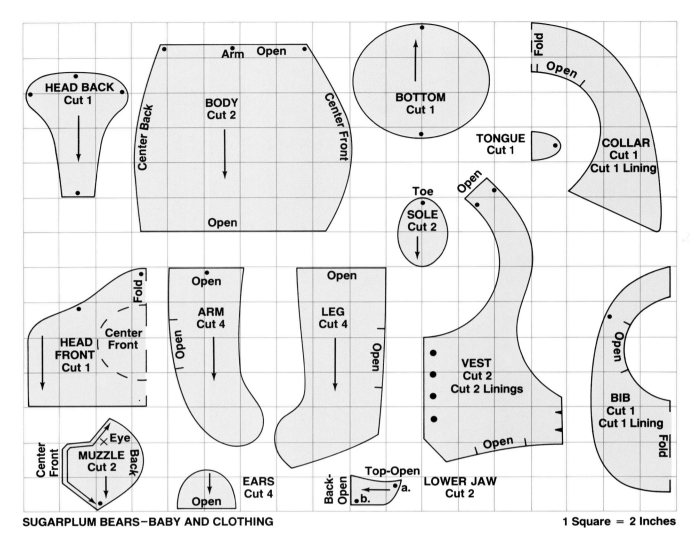

SUGARPLUM BEARS—BABY AND CLOTHING 1 Square = 2 Inches

■ **To make the clothing**

MAMA'S HAT: Cut a 6x44-inch strip from satin or moiré. Fold the strip in half lengthwise. Stitch all three raw edges, leaving an opening for turning. Turn; slip-stitch the opening closed. Tie the satin strip to the hat. Arrange netting as desired and tack to hat.

MAMA'S COLLAR: Sew collar to lining, leaving open as indicated on the pattern. Turn; slip-stitch the opening closed. Sew lace to outer collar edge. Place the collar around the bear's neck; tack collar together at the front edge. Cover a large button with contrasting satin fabric according to the manufacturer's directions; sew on button at front edge.

PAPA'S VEST: Sew the end of a 12-inch-long ribbon to each vest side seam between notches. Sew vest pieces to matching linings, leaving openings as indicated. Turn right side out through the bottom opening; slip-stitch closed.

Sew vest fronts together at back neck, keeping the lining away from stitching. Slip-stitch lining over the seam using small, invisible stitches.

Lap the left front over the right front ½ inch; baste. Cover four buttons in contrasting fabric; sew buttons along vest center front at dots. Slip neckband over bear's head; tie the side ribbons together in back.

PAPA'S TIE: Cut a 5x25-inch piece of satin or moiré. Fold the fabric in half lengthwise. Sew diagonally across each end and along the long side, leaving opening for turning. Turn; blindstitch opening closed. Tie into a bow. Slip ⅛-inch-wide ribbon through the knot; tie the bow around the bear's neck.

BABY'S BIB: Cut a 2½x44-inch strip of satin or moiré. Fold the piece in half lengthwise; sew across the ends. Turn; press. Baste long raw edges together. Pleat the strip to fit the bib between dots. Baste trim to bib, matching right sides and raw edges.

Sew lining to bib, catching the pleated ruffle in the seam and leaving opening on the neck edge as indicated on

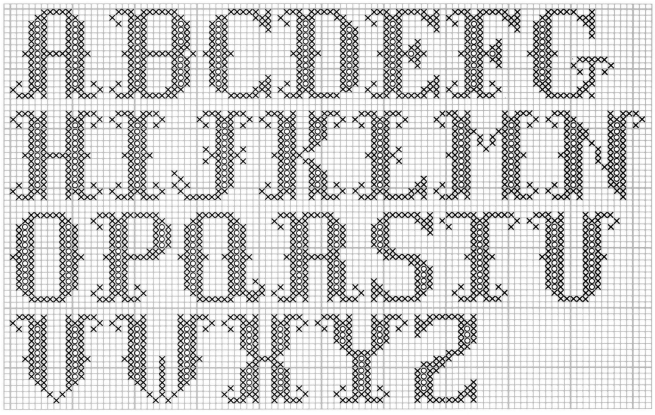

ALPHABET FOR CROSS-STITCHED INITIAL PILLOW

1 Square = 1 Stitch

the pattern. Turn; slip-stitch opening closed. Place the bib around the bear's neck, overlapping the ends at back. Tack the ends together. Tie the neck ribbon around the bear's neck.

Peppermint Garland
Shown on page 8.

MATERIALS
One package *each* of red and white rickrack
Spray starch

INSTRUCTIONS
Intertwine the red rickrack with white rickrack so pieces "braid" together; press to flatten. Machine-stitch lengthwise through the center of the braided piece. Press flat, using spray starch.

Cross-Stitched Initial Pillow
Shown on page 9.
Finished pillow is approximately 9 inches square, excluding the 2½-inch-wide ruffle.

MATERIALS
10x10-inch piece of 10-count Copenhagen fabric or other 10-count even-weave fabric (available through local crafts shops or write to Norden Crafts, P.O. Box 1, 222 Waukegan Road, Glenview, IL 60025)
Embroidery floss in desired color
⅜ yard of striped fabric for pillow back and ruffle
Masking tape
Optional: piping in a color to coordinate with fabric
Polyester fiberfill

INSTRUCTIONS
Bind edges of the cross-stitch fabric with masking tape to prevent raveling. Working with three strands of floss, cross-stitch initial onto the center of the even-weave fabric. Remove tape.

From striped fabric, cut a 10-inch square for the pillow back. From the remaining fabric, cut two 6x32-inch strips for the ruffle.

If desired, baste piping to the seam line around the pillow front.

Join the short ends of the strips to form a long loop. Press the ruffle loop in half, wrong sides facing, so the strip is 3 inches wide. Run a gathering stitch ¼ inch from the raw edge.

Gather and baste one-fourth of the ruffle to each side of the pillow top. With right sides facing and using a ½-inch seam, stitch the front to the back, leaving an opening for turning. Turn and stuff; slip-stitch the opening closed.

Sugarplum Quilt

Shown on page 9.
Finished quilt is approximately
56½x66½ inches.
Finished Double Nine-Patch block is
6¾ inches square.

MATERIALS

1¼ yards of assorted red and dark
   pink fabric scraps
2 yards of pink print for borders and
   binding
9 yards of white or muslin fabric
   (includes quilt backing)
Quilt batting
Cardboard or plastic for templates
Graph paper

INSTRUCTIONS

Unless otherwise stated, ¼-inch seam
allowances are included; sew pieces
with right sides facing. *Note:* The Y and
Z setting triangles *do not* include seam
allowances; be sure to add ¼-inch seam
allowances to these pieces before cutting them from fabric.

MAKING TEMPLATES: Draw a 1¼-
inch square on graph paper for pattern
A, a 2¾-inch square for pattern B, and
a 7¼-inch square for pattern X. Make
templates for squares A, B, and X from
cardboard or plastic.

To make templates for Y and Z setting triangles, draw a 6¾-inch square
on graph paper. Referring to Figure 1,
near right, divide the square into three
triangles. Make templates for Y and Z
triangles. Add ¼-inch seam allowances
to all sides when cutting Y and Z triangles from fabric.

CUTTING: Use template A to cut
875 squares from the assorted red and
pink print fabrics.

Cut two 2-yard-long pieces of muslin for backing. Cut two 2¾-inch-wide
border strips off the side of one of
these panels. Set aside backing and
borders. From the remaining 5 yards
of muslin, use template X to cut 24
setting squares. Using template Y, cut
20 triangles with the long side of the
triangles on the fabric grain. Use template Z to cut four triangles with the
short sides on the fabric grain.

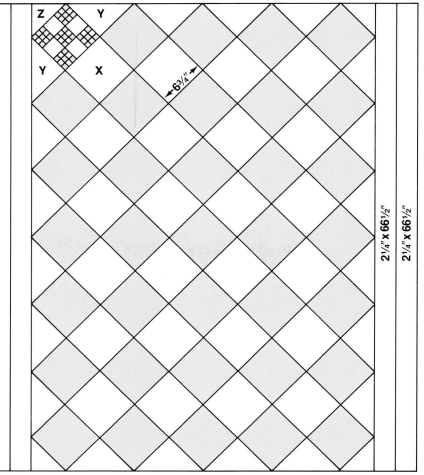

QUILT ASSEMBLY DIAGRAM

From the remaining uncut muslin,
cut 140 squares with template B and
700 squares with template A.

From the pink border and binding
fabric, cut two 2¾-inch-wide border
strips the length of the yardage. Set the
remaining fabric aside for the binding.

PIECING ONE BLOCK: To make a
small Nine-Patch block, refer to Figure
2, *far right,* and lay out five pink A
squares and four white A squares in a
checkerboard. Sew the squares together in rows; join the three rows. Make
175 Nine-Patch blocks.

To make a Double Nine-Patch
block, refer to Figure 2, and combine
five Nine-Patch blocks and four white
B squares.

Piece 35 Double Nine-Patch blocks.

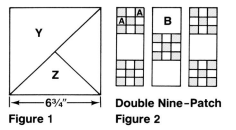

Figure 1

Double Nine-Patch
Figure 2

ASSEMBLING QUILT TOP: Lay out
the 35 pieced blocks, the X setting
squares, the Y setting triangles, and the
Z corner triangles in diagonal rows, as
shown in the assembly diagram, *top.*
Sew the blocks and the setting pieces
together in *diagonal* rows. Combine the
rows to complete the inner quilt top.

For each side border, sew one pink border strip to one white border strip. Sew a completed border strip to each side of the assembled quilt top, with the pink strip to the inside.

FINISHING: Sew the two backing fabric panels together to fit the quilt top. Layer top, batting, and quilt back; baste. Quilt as desired.

From the remaining pink print fabric, cut approximately seven yards of 2¼-inch-wide binding strips. Fold the binding in half lengthwise with the wrong sides together; press.

Sew binding around all edges of the quilt top, matching raw edges and right sides. Trim excess batting and backing. Turn binding over the edge; hand-sew the binding to the quilt back.

Moonbeam Ornament

Shown on page 8.
Finished ornament is 6½ inches high.

MATERIALS
For each ornament
One 3-inch plastic-foam ball
One 2-inch circle of heavy white cardboard
One 7-inch-square piece of white poster board
One 8-inch circle of sheer, shiny white fabric
7 inches of white cording
9 inches of white pearl cotton
White enamel spray paint
Light pink and blue acrylic paint
Glitter snow
Spray adhesive
Sequin pins with flat heads
White glue or hot-melt glue gun and glue sticks
Crafts knife
One small package of white modeling compound

INSTRUCTIONS
Using rolling motions, shape modeling compound into a long, thin strand. For each ornament, shape pieces for eyebrows/nose, a mouth, two eyes and two cheeks according to the pattern, *above right.* Bake the pieces following the manufacturer's directions; cool.

FULL-SIZE PATTERN

MOONBEAM ORNAMENT

Glue the eyebrows/nose and mouth pieces to the small cardboard circle. Let dry; spray with white enamel.

Using acrylic paint, paint molded eye pieces light blue and cheek pieces pale pink. Let dry; glue to the cardboard circle.

Spray the cardboard face with spray adhesive; sprinkle with glitter snow. Set aside.

Cut a 2-inch circle from paper; pin to foam ball. Trace around the circle onto the ball; remove paper. With a serrated knife, cut off this portion so the ball has a flat side. With the flat side facing up, center the ball on the sheer fabric circle. Pull the fabric edges onto the flat portion of the ball; gather or pleat the fabric as it goes over the flat edges. Pin fabric to ball with sequin pins. Glue the cardboard face over the flat surface, covering the pins and raw edges.

continued

Trace the moonbeam shape on page 17 onto tracing paper; cut out pattern. Trace around the moonbeam shape onto poster board; cut out using crafts knife. Cut out center opening on the moonbeam. Slip the moonbeam over the plastic ball face. Glue cording around the edge of the cardboard face.

To create a hanger for the ornament, fold the pearl cotton in half; tie ends. Using a sequin pin dipped in glue, secure the hanger to the ornament, pinning it ½ inch behind the corded face edge.

Candy Wreath

Shown on page 9.
Finished size is approximately 11 inches in diameter.

MATERIALS

10½-inch round foam wreath form
Crafts glue or hot-melt glue gun
Assorted hard candies
High-gloss spray polyurethane
Thin wire

INSTRUCTIONS

Working in small sections, glue candy to the wreath form, layering and overlapping the candy pieces as necessary to completely cover the wreath form. Work to balance the candy colors and to create an even, circular shape.

When the wreath is completely dry, apply several coats of polyurethane, letting dry completely between coats.

Attach wire to the back of the wreath form; bend the wire into a loop to hang the wreath.

Ballerina Doll

Shown on page 10.
Finished size is approximately 24½ inches tall.

MATERIALS

½ yard muslin for head, arms, body
½ yard of shiny knit for legs
½ yard of stretch knit for leotard
¾ yard of satin for skirt
Scrap of satin for shoes
Dark gray and bright pink embroidery floss
Jewel-like bead for necklace
2 yards of ½-inch-wide satin ribbon for slipper lacing
1 yard of ⅛-inch-wide satin ribbon for slipper bows
1 yard of ½-inch-wide satin ribbon for skirt ties and necklace
1½ yards *each* of four different colors of ⅛-inch-wide satin ribbon for hair bows
Two yards of hemp rope for hair
Assorted dried flowers
Glittered baby's-breath
Satin rosettes and fabric flower clusters for headpiece
Florist's wire
Powdered blush
Three small snap fasteners
Polyester fiberfill
Old brush or comb
Dressmaker's carbon paper
Doll needle and carpet thread
Graph paper

INSTRUCTIONS

Note: Unless otherwise stated, ¼-inch seam allowances are included on all patterns and cutting instructions; sew all pieces with right sides together.

Enlarge the patterns, *opposite,* onto graph paper. If you take the pattern to a store or company that does enlargements, ask to have the patterns enlarged 267 percent. Cut all patterns from appropriate fabrics.

FACE AND HEAD: Using dressmaker's carbon paper, lightly transfer all face markings onto face. Referring to stitch diagrams on page 156, outline-stitch the eyebrows, eye outlines, and nose, using four strands of gray floss. Satin-stitch the eyes with gray floss. Outline-stitch two rows of pink floss for the mouth. Brush on powdered blush for the cheeks.

Sew the head front to the head back, leaving open at neck. Stuff the head firmly; set aside.

ARMS AND LEGS: Narrowly hem the top edge of the four slipper pieces. Baste the slippers to the foot of the leg pieces, matching raw edges and having wrong side of slipper facing right side of foot. Hand-sew or machine-top-stitch the hemmed edge of the slippers to the foot along the hemline.

Sew legs and arms together in pairs, leaving open at the top. Turn to right side; stuff firmly. Set aside.

BODY: Sew body front to body back, leaving open at neck. Turn and stuff firmly. Fold neck edge of head under along the dashed line as indicated; slip the head over the neck of body and hand-sew in place. Before closing the neck, add extra fiberfill as necessary to keep the head erect. Hand-sew neck ribbon around the neck, concealing the neck seam.

Turn upper edge of legs under along dashed lines. Using a doll needle and carpet thread, hand-sew the legs to the body at the leg markings, positioning the legs so the toes point inward. Add extra fiberfill as needed before closing the seam. Attach the arms in the same manner, positioning the arms so the thumbs point inward.

SLIPPERS: Cut ribbon for the slipper lacings in half. Tack the center of one piece to the center back of one slipper. Repeat for the other slipper. Crisscross the ribbons around the legs from front to back, wrapping the ribbons to knee level. Tie the ribbons in a bow at the side of the legs; tack in place.

Cut the ribbon for the slipper bows in half. Tie each ribbon in a bow; tack a bow to each slipper. Trim the ribbon ends to the desired length.

LEOTARD: Sew center back seam from crotch to dot. Narrowly hem the edges of the center back opening.

Sew front to back at shoulders. Narrowly hem leg and neck edges.

Sew the sleeves together in pairs along the outer curved edges. Sew the sleeves to the arm openings, matching the sleeve seam with the shoulder

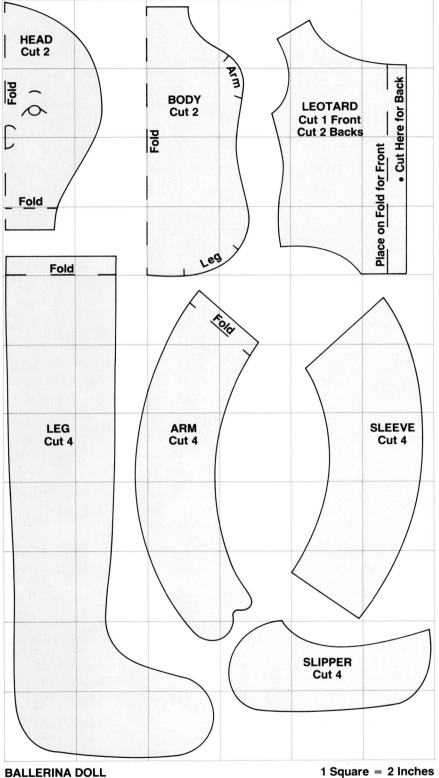

HEAD
Cut 2

Fold

Fold

BODY
Cut 2

Fold

Arm

Leg

LEOTARD
Cut 1 Front
Cut 2 Backs

Place on Fold for Front

• Cut Here for Back

Fold

LEG
Cut 4

Fold

ARM
Cut 4

SLEEVE
Cut 4

SLIPPER
Cut 4

BALLERINA DOLL

1 Square = 2 Inches

seam. Sew each sleeve and side seam in one continuous seam. Sew the crotch seam. Hem the sleeves.

Sew two snaps to the back opening. Tack bead at the center front.

SKIRT: Cut a 24-inch circle from the skirt fabric. Cut a 3½-inch circle from the center for the waist. Slash the skirt from the waist to the bottom to make an opening. Curve the corners of the skirt at the opening along the hemline.

Narrowly hem all skirt edges except the waistline. From the remaining skirt fabric, cut a 1x14-inch binding strip. Bind the waist edge with the binding strip, encasing the raw edges; trim the binding strip to fit the waist.

Place the skirt on the doll, overlapping the skirt slightly at the waistline opening. Sew a snap to the waist edge so the underlap is secure and the overlap remains free.

Cut the skirt ribbon in half. Tack a ribbon to the skirt overlap edge and the waistband; tie the ribbon to secure the skirt overlap. Tack flower at the base of the ribbon.

HAIR: Cut hemp in half, then unravel it into single strands. Comb through the hemp with an old brush or comb to soften and straighten the strands. Lay strands out flat so the center is approximately 6 inches wide. Sew across the center several times to secure strands and to create a part in the hair.

Position the hair on the doll's head and tack in place. Trim the ends and cut bangs as desired.

HEADPIECE: Cut a 20-inch piece of florist's wire for the base. Wire small clusters of baby's-breath and dried flowers to the base wire, leaving the ends free. Add fabric flower clusters, dried flowers, and satin rosettes. Shape the wire into circle to fit on the doll's head and join the ends. Tie the hair ribbons into one bow, leaving long tails. Wire the bow over the joined ends of the headpiece. Tack the headpiece in place on the doll's head.

Toy Soldier Doll

Shown on page 10.
Finished doll is 26 inches tall.

MATERIALS

½ yard of dark red fabric for the body, arms, and jacket
9½x23-inch piece of muslin for the head and hands
10x20-inch piece of blue fabric for the legs
7x30-inch piece of black fabric for the boots
7½x18-inch piece of black fur for hat
Brown yarn for hair
Blue, flesh, dark rust, white, and dark red embroidery floss
Four ¾-inch-diameter dark red buttons for the joints
Eight ½-inch-diameter gold buttons for the jacket and hat
1½ yards of ⅜-inch-wide green or striped grosgrain ribbon
Eight small gold beads
¾ yard of ⅝-inch-wide double-fold black polyester braid
One small gold D-ring
½ yard of ¼-inch-wide black satin ribbon
One ¾-inch-diameter gold metal button with emblem
½ yard of gold braid for hat
½ yard of gold upholstery fringe
Powdered blush
Polyester fiberfill
Buttonhole twist
Doll needle
Dressmaker's carbon paper
Graph paper

INSTRUCTIONS

Note: Unless otherwise stated, ¼-inch seam allowances are included on all patterns and cutting instructions; sew pieces with right sides together.

Enlarge the patterns, *opposite,* onto graph paper. If you take the pattern to an enlargement company, ask them to enlarge the pattern to 308 percent. Cut patterns from appropriate fabrics.

In addition to the patterns, cut two 7¼x3½-inch pieces for cuffs and one 8½x22-inch piece for the jacket bottom from the red fabric. From black fabric, cut two 3x8-inch boot cuffs.

BODY: Sew center front and center back seams. Sew front to back, leaving the neck open. Turn and stuff till firm.

FACE: Using dressmaker's carbon paper, transfer the facial details to the face. Using two strands of embroidery floss for all embroidery, and referring to the stitch diagrams on page 156, satin-stitch the eyes with blue floss and the nose with flesh floss. Straight-stitch the eyelashes using dark rust floss and the eye dots with white floss. Stem-stitch the smile with dark red floss. Color the cheeks with powdered blush.

HEAD: Join the head back pieces along the center seam. Sew the chin to the face, matching centers and dots. Sew the face to the head back from dot to dot along the top of the head. Sew the head back to the chin from each dot to neck, easing to fit. Turn; stuff head till firm. Turn under the raw edges along the neck. Slip-stitch the head to the body, using a doll needle.

HAIR: Wrap yarn around four fingers 15 times. Tie one end of the loops with yarn; cut the other end. Repeat, making 15 bunches. Tack the bunches around the face and to the lower section of the head. Trim ends as desired.

LEGS: Sew green or striped ribbon along fold line of two legs to form the stripe on the pants. Sew one boot top to bottom of each leg, reversing two boot pieces to make right and left pairs.

Sew the legs together in pairs, leaving openings as indicated. Sew one sole to each boot, matching centers. Clip the curves, turn, and stuff, keeping the top of the legs slightly flat. Slip-stitch the opening closed.

Fold each boot cuff in half lengthwise; stitch around the raw edges, leaving an opening for turning. Turn; slip-stitch opening closed. Tack a cuff to each boot, matching the ends at the top of the boot on the outside of the leg.

For the bootstraps, cut the black ribbon in two equal lengths. Fold each ribbon in half, and tack the ends to the top and back of each boot.

Form a length of upholstery fringe into two tassels; tack a tassel to the center front of each boot; sew a small gold bead above each tassel.

To join legs to body, match the X marking on one leg to the X marking on one side of the body. Using a doll needle and buttonhole twist, sew from one side through the body, leg top, and a button, and back through the body. Repeat the back and forth stitching several times to firmly attach a leg. Repeat for the other leg.

JACKET: Fold the jacket bottom in half lengthwise; sew together each short end. Turn right side out; fit the raw edge around the doll waist, allowing a 1-inch overlap at the center front. Form a small pleat at each side and an inverted pleat at the center back; pin pleats. Remove jacket bottom from the doll; machine-baste the pleat tops.

Encase the raw edge of the jacket waist with black double-fold braid, turning under the braid ends. Tack the braid to doll's waist. Tack a D-ring to the braid at center front for a buckle.

For the collar, from red fabric cut a 1½-inch-wide bias strip ½ inch longer than the measurement of the doll's neck. Fold the collar in half lengthwise. Sew the raw edges together, leaving an opening for turning. Turn; slip-stitch opening. Place the collar around the doll's neck with the ends at the center front. Slip-stitch the ends together; tack collar to doll's neck.

Sew epaulets together in pairs. Slash one side of each pair. Turn right side out through the slash; whipstitch slash closed. Tack fringe around the curved edges. Tack epaulets to shoulders.

Sew three gold buttons to the body on each side of the front.

ARMS: Sew a hand to each arm, reversing two hands to make the pairs. Sew the arms together in pairs, leaving open as indicated on the pattern. Restitch the thumb area to reinforce it; clip, and turn. Stuff, keeping the top of the arms slightly flat. Slip-stitch the opening closed.

With wrong sides together, fold each cuff in half lengthwise; press. Cut four 7¼-inch lengths of the green or striped ribbon. On each cuff, topstitch one ribbon at the fold edge and another across the top, covering raw edges.

Sew the short sides of the cuff together, forming a ring. Slip the cuff

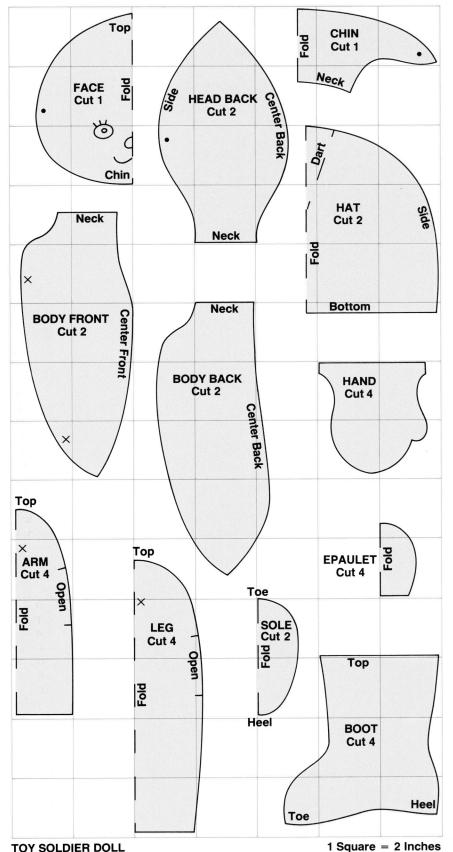

over the hand; tack the top edge of the ribbon to one arm, matching the cuff seam to the back arm seam.

Sew three gold beads to the outside of each cuff, one on each ribbon and one at the center.

Join the arms to the body in the same manner as the legs.

HAT: Sew the hat darts; trim the darts. Sew the hat pieces together, leaving the bottom open. Turn the bottom edge under; hem. Slip-stitch gold braid to the lower edge.

Cut 10½ inches of double-fold braid for the hat strap. Tack the ends of the straps to the hat sides. Sew a gold button to the hat at each end of the strap.

Form a short length of upholstery fringe into a tassel; tack the tassel to the center top of the hat. Sew the emblem button to the hat at the top of the tassel. Tack the hat to the doll's head.

Needlepoint Gingerbread House

Shown on page 11.
Finished house is approximately 11½ inches tall.

MATERIALS

Paternayan Persian yarn in the
following colors:
  350 strands of brown (No. 433)
  150 strands of white (No. 260)
  40 strands of yellow (No. 711)
  16 strands light green (No. 634)
  36 strands *each* of pink (No. 945),
    dark green (No. 633), and
    red (No. 971)
  10 strands *each* of orange
    (No. 812), aqua (No. 584),
    and light yellow (No. 712)
Six sheets of No. 7 brown plastic
  needlepoint canvas
No. 16 plastic canvas needles
Optional: foam-core mounting board,
  beads, trim, ⅜-inch-diameter
  dowel, red acrylic paint

INSTRUCTIONS

Note: All work is done using two strands of yarn, except the border finishing, which uses only one strand. Unless directed otherwise, work all areas with the continental stitch.

continued

TOY SOLDIER DOLL   1 Square = 2 Inches

STITCHING: Stitch the house pieces before cutting the canvas. Work larger pieces first, then use scraps for the smaller ones. Leave at least one row of unworked squares around each shape; these are used to assemble the pieces.

Stitch all the pieces following the charts, *right* and *opposite,* noting the following instructions.

To stitch the roof, work all the white outlining stitches first. Stitch the brown "tiles" with designs next. Using brown yarn, fill in remaining "tiles" with upright gobelin stitches (see diagram, page 157). Work the chimney in four adjacent sections as shown, leaving at least two squares between sections so they can be cut apart.

Cut each shape out of the plastic, leaving one square intact on all sides. Cut the chimney as four pieces.

Decorate each house piece with beads and sequins as desired.

ASSEMBLY: Finish tops and bottoms of the house back, front, and two sides by working long-legged cross-stitches with one strand of white yarn along the edges of the pieces. Using the same stitch, join these house sections.

In the same manner, finish the side and lower edges of the roof pieces. Join roof pieces at the top edges.

Join all four chimney pieces in a row as indicated on chart, leaving the final seam open. Lay chimney flat; finish chimney top and bottom edges in the same manner as for the house pieces. Sew final chimney seam.

Referring to the photograph on page 11 for position, attach chimney to roof with small needlepoint stitches.

If desired, cut a dowel to the length of the rooftop; paint dowel red. Wrap the dowel with red and white yarns in candy-cane fashion, gluing the yarn as you twist. Glue the covered dowel along the peak of the roof.

Position the roof atop the house; stitch roof to house pieces. If desired, place polyester fiberfill "smoke" in chimney, and glue lace along the edges of the roof.

If you need added stability for the house, cut pieces of foam-core board to correspond to the house pieces. Do not cut pieces for the chimney. Assemble the board house, then slip the needlepoint house over it.

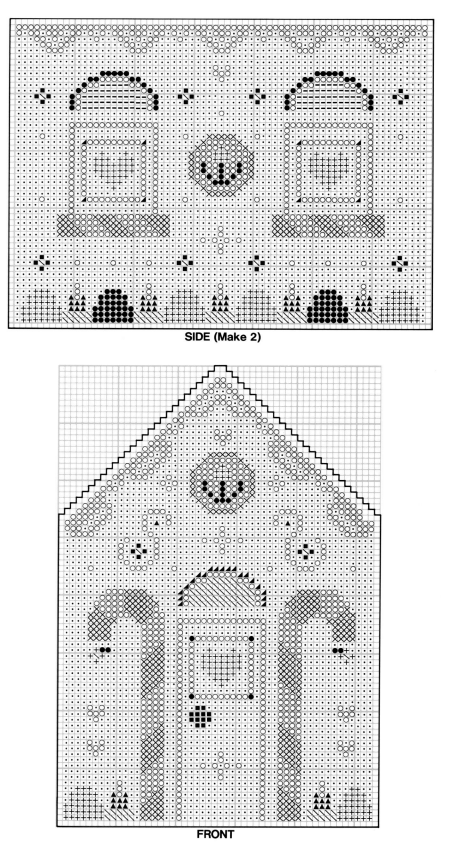

SIDE (Make 2)

FRONT
NEEDLEPOINT GINGERBREAD HOUSE

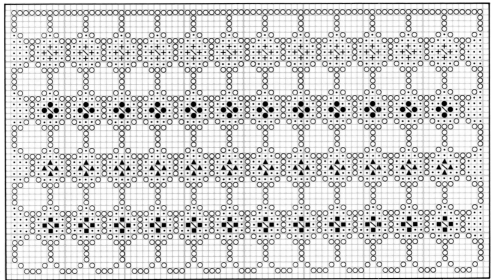

ROOF (Make 2)

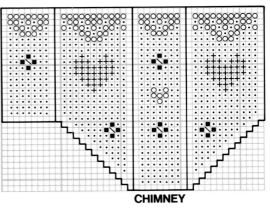

CHIMNEY

BACK

COLOR KEY

⊠	Red	▲	Orange
⊙	White	⊞	Pink
·	Brown	⊟	Lt. Green
◥	Lt. Yellow	●	Dk. Green
◢	Dk. Yellow	■	Turquoise

23

All Creatures
Great and Small

Since the first Christmas, endearing animals have played an important role in holiday festivities. Crafted little creatures are especially heartwarming for special young friends.

A holiday ribbon puts Barney Bear, *opposite,* in the spirit. Knitted in one piece with double-pointed needles, the shaping techniques are borrowed from those for socks and other common shapes. Directions are on page 37.

Little ones will love the doll or bear at *left*—both machine-stitched from purchased socks—or the crocheted lamb. Directions for stuffed toys begin on page 33.

The cheery "creature comforts" of animals bring warmth and brightness to a holiday home, so surely your crafted Christmas gifts will be dearly loved throughout the years.

Cat fanciers will find the clever stitchery *above* simply irresistible. The sampler features eight felines cross-stitched in a grid border around the heart-felt message.

The finished piece is 5¼ inches square worked on 14-count Aida cloth. The sampler graph and instructions are on page 32.

Even cat lovers will enjoy this clan of long-tailed Christmas mice, *right*. Stitched from a basic pattern, each

wears simple-to-sew clothing that gives Papa, Sonny, Mama, Grandpa, and Baby a unique identity. Add details with ties, eyeglasses, buttons, or tiny packages.

The mice are made of gray knit fabric and are weighted at the bottom with washers. The weight of each mouse is about ¾ pound—heavy enough to support a stocking of holiday treats of equal weight. Coat-hanger wire, slipped into the fabric tails, stiffens the tails for holding stockings.

Full-size patterns and directions for Mouse Stocking Hangers begin on page 28.

Mouse Stocking Hangers

Shown on pages 26 and 27. Finished mice are 5¼, 5¾, and 6½ inches tall.

MATERIALS

■ Bodies
½ yard of 45-inch-wide gray knit fabric for mouse bodies
Polyester fiberfill
Black button warp for whiskers
Black embroidery floss
Five coat hangers
½-inch eye from hook-and-eye set for glasses
Five 2½-inch circles cut from 1-inch pine for base
Forty 2-inch-diameter washers (total weight 4 pounds)
Sewing thread

■ Clothing
Papa's clothing
9x12-inch piece of knit fabric for sweater
Two ⅜-inch-diameter buttons

Mama's clothing
5-inch length of silver chain
5x13-inch piece of print fabric for apron
⅔ yard of ⅛-inch-wide ribbon to match print fabric
6½ inches of ¼-inch-wide elastic

Grandpa's clothing
11x12-inch blue velvet fabric for jacket
Three gold sequins
Two ½x10-inch strips of white fabric for ascot

Sonny's clothing
10-inch square of white fabric for shirt
Scrap of red print fabric for tie

Baby's clothing
5 inches of 3¾-inch-wide white gathered eyelet for dress
Two 2½-inch lengths of 1-inch-wide gathered eyelet for sleeves
⅓ yard of ⅛-inch-wide silver braid

INSTRUCTIONS

Note: All patterns and measurements include ¼-inch seam allowances. Sew the seams with the right sides of the fabric facing. Carefully clip the curved seam allowances, and press the seams open where possible.

Trace the patterns on pages 29–31. Cut out pieces from fabrics as indicated in the materials list.

In addition, cut two arms for each mouse from the gray knit fabric. Use the following measurements for each pair of arms: 1½x4 inches (adult), 1½x3½ inches (boy), and 1½x3 inches (baby). Use the remaining gray knit to cut a 1½x13-inch tail for each mouse.

From the print fabric, cut one 5x11-inch rectangle (apron skirt) and two 2x2½-inch rectangles (apron bib).

■ Mice Bodies
BASE: Drill a 1⅛-inch-deep hole in the *side* of each wooden base. Straighten the coat hangers; cut each to 26 inches long. Bend the hangers in half, and insert the cut ends into the holes in the base for the tails.

Referring to the base diagram, *below,* bend the tails halfway around the base toward the front and straight out 1½

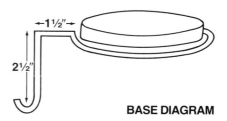

BASE DIAGRAM

inches. Then bend the wire down for 2½ inches; bend the tips upward to form hooks.

BODY: Sew the center front seam. Sew the back to the front along the sides. Stitch the bottom circle to the bottom edge of the body leaving the front open. Turn the body right side out; stuff the upper body, leaving the bottom 3 inches unstuffed.

Cut a ¼-inch-long slit in the center back ½ inch above the bottom seam. Stack washers atop pine base and push them into the bottom of the mouse through the front opening. From inside, push the wire tail end out through

the back slit. Continue stuffing around the washers until body is smooth and round; sew front opening closed.

Fold the tail fabric in half lengthwise; sew along the long edge and one short edge. Turn right side out; slip tail over wire. Hand-sew the end to body.

HEAD: Fold the head forward along the neckline, 1¾ inches from the tip of the nose. Slip-stitch under the chin to secure the head in place.

Satin-stitch the eyes and a nose with two strands of black embroidery floss. Thread two 1¾-inch-long strands of black button warp through the top of the nose for the whiskers.

EARS: Sew the ear fronts to the backs, leaving openings between dots. Turn the ears right side out. Fold the raw edges under; stitch the ears in place approximately 2 inches from the nose.

FEET: Sew pairs of foot pieces together, leaving openings between dots. Turn; stuff lightly. Stitch along toe lines, indicated by dashed lines on the pattern. Turn the raw edges under; stitch the feet to the body front.

■ Clothing
PAPA'S SWEATER: Sew the sweater fronts to back at shoulders. Sew sleeves to sweater body; stitch underarm/side seams. Turn under ¼ inch along the sweater bottom raw edge; hem.

Put the sweater on the mouse; lap the left front opening over the right front opening. Secure the openings with wooden buttons.

MAMA'S APRON: Sew two 2x2½-inch apron bib rectangles together leaving one long side unstitched; turn.

Turn under ¼ inch twice along each long edge of the 5x11-inch rectangle to make hems; stitch. Beginning ½ inch from the bottom hemmed edge, stitch three ⅛-inch tucks ¼ inch apart across the length of the fabric. Fold under ¼ inch twice along each short edge to make hems; stitch. Stretch and sew elastic to top edge of apron.

Align the raw edges of the bib with center top edge of the apron skirt; stitch. Stitch 4½-inch-long ribbon ties to the bib top and 5-inch-long ribbon ties to the skirt sides.

GRANDPA'S JACKET: Sew fronts to back along the sleeve/shoulder seams. Fold sleeve bottom and front opening edges under ½ inch; topstitch to hem.

Press under ¼ inch on all sides of the pocket; topstitch ⅛ inch from the top edge. Sew pocket on jacket front.

Turn the jacket bottom edge under ¼ inch; hem. Sew the collar front to the collar back leaving the bottom edge unstitched; turn. Pin collar to the jacket neck with raw edges even; stitch.

Put jacket on mouse, lapping front edges; slip-stitch jacket closed. Trim jacket front with gold sequin buttons.

For the ascot, turn under ⅛ inch along each edge of ascot to make hems; stitch. Wrap the ascot around Grandpa's neck.

SONNY'S SHIRT AND TIE: Repeat as for Grandpa's jacket omitting the pocket and the buttons.

Sew two tie pieces together, leaving top open for turning. Turn; sew the opening closed; press. Tie a knot in the top of the tie; tuck the tie under the collar and hand-stitch in place.

BABY'S DRESS: Center two ¾-inch buttonholes 3 inches apart and ¾ inch down from the top edge of the 3¾-inch-wide eyelet to form armholes. Slip dress on mouse, with the opening at the back. Turn one opening edge under ¼ inch; lap over the remaining edge; slip-stitch the dress back closed.

Fold each 1-inch-wide eyelet strip in half, widthwise; sew along the short edge for sleeves. Turn sleeves right side out. Slip the sleeves over the arms; slip-stitch to dress.

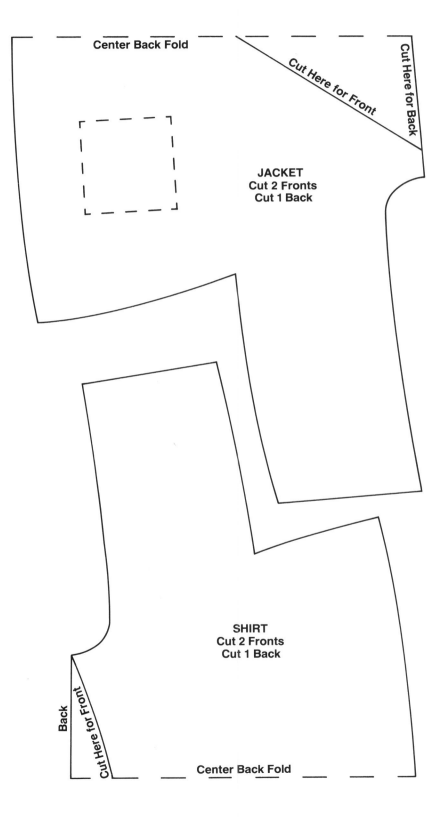

Center Back Fold

Cut Here for Front

Cut Here for Back

JACKET
Cut 2 Fronts
Cut 1 Back

SHIRT
Cut 2 Fronts
Cut 1 Back

Back

Cut Here for Front

Center Back Fold

JACKET POCKET
Cut 2

MOUSE STOCKING HANGERS

29

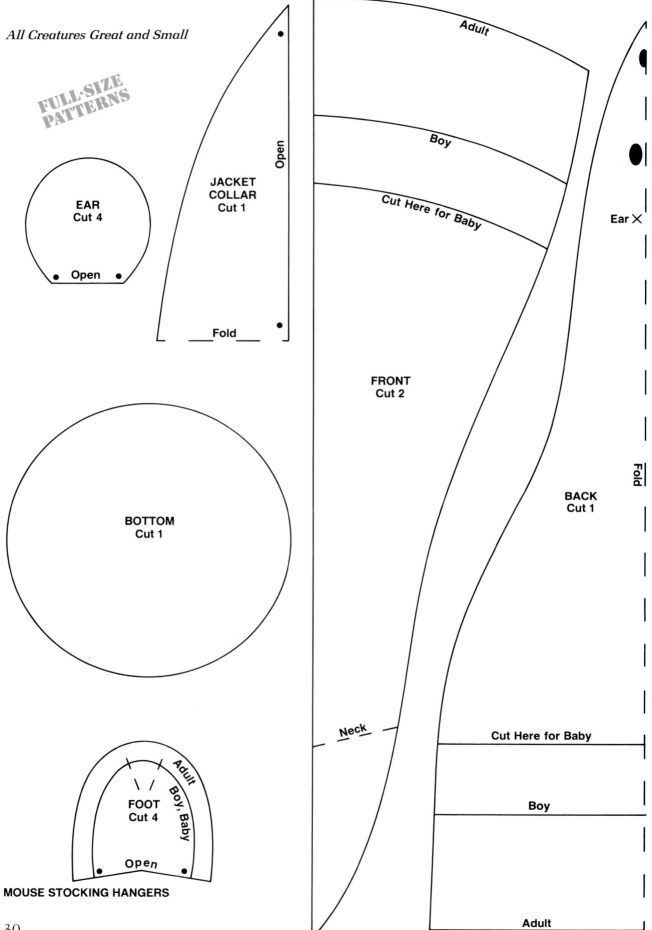

All Creatures Great and Small

FULL·SIZE
PATTERNS

EAR
Cut 4

Open

JACKET
COLLAR
Cut 1

Open

Fold

Adult

Boy

Cut Here for Baby

FRONT
Cut 2

Ear ✕

Fold

BACK
Cut 1

BOTTOM
Cut 1

Neck

Cut Here for Baby

Boy

Adult
Boy, Baby

FOOT
Cut 4

Open

MOUSE STOCKING HANGERS

Adult

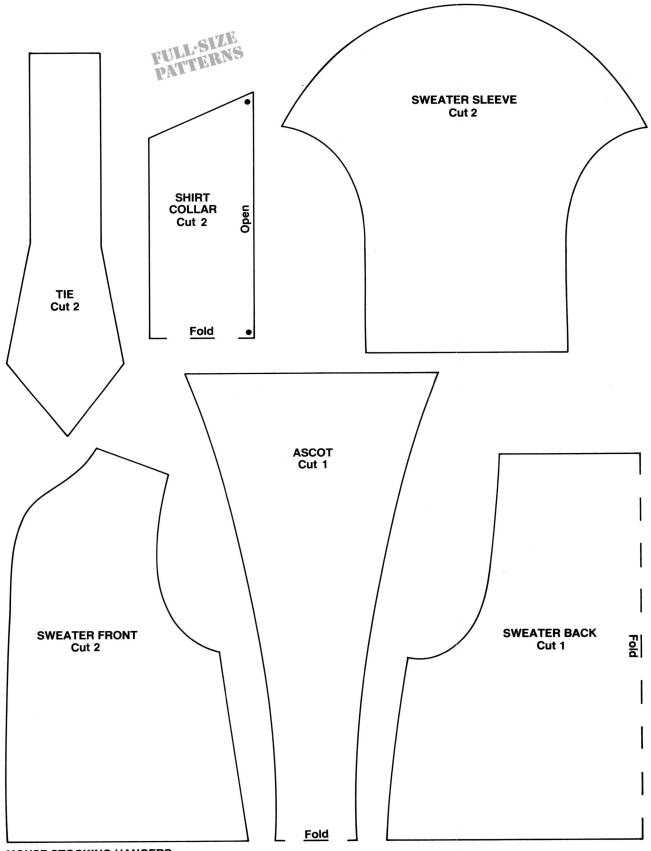

FULL-SIZE PATTERNS

TIE
Cut 2

SHIRT
COLLAR
Cut 2

Open

Fold

SWEATER SLEEVE
Cut 2

ASCOT
Cut 1

SWEATER FRONT
Cut 2

SWEATER BACK
Cut 1

Fold

Fold

MOUSE STOCKING HANGERS

31

Cross-Stitched Cats

Shown on page 26.
Finished stitchery is about 5¼x5½ inches.
Stitch count is 69 wide and 75 high.

MATERIALS

10x10-inch piece of 14-count ivory
    Aida cloth
One skein *each* of DMC embroidery
    floss in the following colors: dark
    blue (311), tan (612), blue (926),
    and pink (3350)
Embroidery hoop
Tapestry needle
Graph paper
Colored marking pens

INSTRUCTIONS

Only a partial pattern is given, *below left,* for the design. Use colored pens to chart the complete design onto graph paper, referring to the photograph on page 26 for guidance.

Using two strands of floss, work cross-stitches over one square of the fabric. Work blue cats in the corner blocks and tan cats in the blocks between the blue cats. Work the letters and hearts in the center block. When the cross-stitching is complete, backstitch the mouths and whiskers on the cats in dark blue with one strand of floss. Frame as desired.

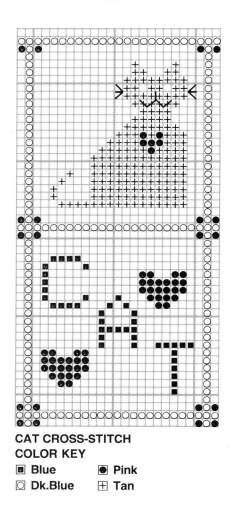

CAT CROSS-STITCH
COLOR KEY

◧ **Blue**   ◓ **Pink**
◪ **Dk.Blue** ⊞ **Tan**

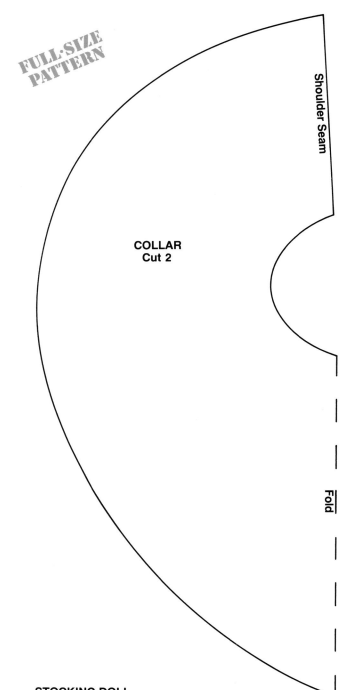

FULL-SIZE PATTERN

Shoulder Seam

COLLAR
Cut 2

Fold

STOCKING DOLL

Stocking Doll

Shown on page 24.
Finished doll is 14 inches tall.

MATERIALS

One pair of women's ivory anklets
½ yard of peach fabric
⅛ yard of green fabric for collar
Two 1x18-inch red fabric strips for hair bows
One 2-ounce skein of 4-ply light brown cotton yarn
Five ⅜-inch-diameter buttons for eyes and collar
⅓ yard of ¼-inch-wide elastic
Red colored pencil
Polyester fiberfill
Four ¼-inch snaps
Cardboard

INSTRUCTIONS

Note: The patterns and measurements include ¼-inch seam allowances unless otherwise indicated. Sew the seams with right sides of the fabric facing.

Trace the doll clothing patterns, *below right* and *opposite*. Pin pattern pieces to the appropriate fabrics and cut out. For the blouse, cut one front piece on the fold of the fabric and two separate back pieces, as the pattern indicates.

In addition, cut a 7½x32-inch skirt and two 3½x32-inch pieces for the skirt ruffle from the peach fabric.

HEAD/BODY: Referring to the sock diagram, *below,* cut off one sock 3 inches above heel. Cut off the toe at stitched toe line; stitch toe opening closed. (Heel section is doll's head.)

Stuff the bottom 5 inches of the sock section to measure 8 inches in circumference. Stuff the heel to round out the head. (The diagonal heel lines should run from the mouth area upward to each side of the doll's cheeks.)

Gather the top edge of the head, pull to the center, and sew closed. Hand-stitch around the neck to define the doll's neck; take tucks in the head to achieve the desired face shape.

FACIAL DETAILS: Sew on button eyes in the positions indicated by a dot on the sock diagram. Draw rosy cheeks with a red pencil.

HAIR: Wrap yarn around a 6-inch-wide piece of cardboard 75 times; cut
continued

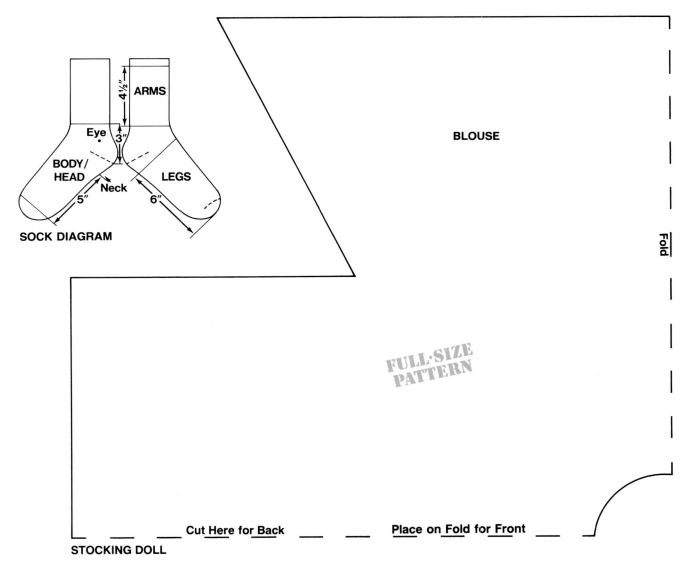

one end of the yarn to make 12-inch-long strands.

Center the yarn on the doll's head. Spread yarn strands evenly from the forehead to the neck to make a center part; whipstitch the strands to the doll's head along the part. Sew yarn to doll's head at ear level. Braid remaining yarn; tie braids with fabric bows.

LEGS: Referring to the sock diagram, cut a 6-inch length from the foot of the second sock. Cut up the center front and the center back of this section to make two pieces.

Sew each piece together forming legs, tapering each doll's foot at the toe stitching line and leaving other end open for turning. Turn legs right side out; stuff; slip-stitch legs to body.

ARMS: Cut a 4½-inch length from the remainder of the second sock. Repeat as for the legs to form arms. Turn, stuff, and sew to body.

SKIRT: Join the skirt ruffle pieces into one long piece. Finish one long edge of the skirt ruffle with a narrow hem. Gather the other long edge to fit one long edge of the skirt rectangle; sew the ruffle to the skirt.

Sew the side seams of the skirt. Press under ¼ inch along the waist edge; fold over again ¾ inch; press. Cut elastic to fit the doll's waist; sew the elastic ends together. Stitch the elastic to the inside of the waistband.

BLOUSE: Serge or machine-zigzag the neck, sleeve, and back opening edges to finish.

Stitch underarm/side seams. Sew snaps in place along the center back opening. Wrap strong thread around the doll's wrists over the sleeves to form sleeve ruffles. Tie the thread to secure the fabric.

COLLAR: Sew the collar front to the collar backs at shoulders. Finish the outer edge of the collar and back opening edges with serged or narrow hems.

Gather neck edge to measure 5½ inches. Cut a light green 1¼x6½-inch bias strip. Pin the bias strip to the gathered neck edge, extending the strip ends ½ inch beyond the back edges; stitch. Press under ¼ inch along bias

raw edge. Fold strip ends and pressed edge to inside; whipstitch to seam line.

Sew buttons in place on collar front.

Crocheted Lamb

Shown on page 24.
Finished size is 12 inches tall.

MATERIALS
3-ply sport-weight yarn (2-ounce skeins): two skeins of white and small amount of black
Size F aluminum crochet hook or size to reach gauge given below
Polyester fiberfill

Abbreviations: See page 35.
Gauge: Over dc, 5 sts = 1 inch; 3 rows = 1 inch.

INSTRUCTIONS
POPCORN (pc): 5 dc in next st, drop hook from lp, insert hook in first dc, pick up dropped lp and draw lp through st on hook, ch 1. *Note:* Popcorns tend to fall to back side of work. When worked on right-side rows, they can be pushed to right side of work.

CENTER SECTION: With white, beg at chest bet front legs, ch 4.
Row 1: Sc in second ch from hook and in each rem ch—3 sc; ch 3, turn.
Row 2: Pc in second sc, dc in next sc; ch 1, turn.
Row 3: Sc in dc, sc in top of pc and in top of turning ch-3; ch 3, turn.
Row 4: Dc in first sc, pc in next sc, 2 dc in next sc; ch 1, turn.
Row 5: Sc in next 2 dc, sc in pc, sc in next dc, sc in top of turning-ch—5 sts; ch 3, turn.
Row 6: 2 dc in first sc, sk next sc, pc in next sc, sk sc, 3 dc in last sc—7 sts; ch 1, turn.
Row 7: Sc in 3 dc, sc in pc, sc in 2 dc, sc in top of turning-ch; ch 3, turn.
Row 8: 2 dc in first sc, pc in next sc, sk sc, 3 dc in next sc, sk sc, pc in next sc, 3 dc in last sc—11 sts; ch 1, turn.
Row 9: Sc in each dc and pc across, sc in top of turning-ch; ch 3, turn.
Row 10: Pc in second sc, (sk sc, 3 dc in next sc, sk sc, pc in next sc) twice, dc in next sc; ch 1, turn.
Row 11: Rep Row 9.

Row 12: 3 dc in second sc, (sk sc, pc in next sc, sk sc, 3 dc in next sc) twice, dc in last sc—13 sts; ch 1, turn.
Row 13: Rep Row 9.
Row 14: Dc in first sc, (sk sc, pc in next sc, sk sc, 3 dc in next sc) twice, sk sc, pc in next sc, sk sc, 2 dc in last sc; ch 1, turn.
Row 15: Rep Row 9.
Row 16: Sk first 2 sc, (3 dc in next sc, sk sc, pc in next sc, sk sc) twice, 3 dc in next sc, sk sc, dc in last sc; ch 1, turn.
Rows 17–20: Rep rows 13–16, omitting ch 1 at end of Row 20.

FIRST SIDE SECTION: *Row 21:* Working down side of piece, ch 3, dc over side of Row 20, pc over side of Row 19, (3 dc over dc at side of next row, pc over sc at side of next row) 5 times, 2 dc over side of Row 8—25 sts; ch 1, turn.
Row 22: Rep Row 9.
Row 23: Sk first 2 sc, (3 dc in next sc, sk sc, pc in next sc, sk sc) 5 times; 3 dc in next sc, sk sc, dc in last sc; ch 1, turn.
Row 24: Rep Row 9.
Row 25: Dc in first sc, (sk sc, pc in next sc, sk sc, 3 dc in next sc) 5 times, sk sc, pc in next sc, sk sc, 2 dc in last sc; ch 1, turn.
Row 26: Rep Row 9.
Row 27: Rep Row 23, omitting ch 1 at end of row; ch 7, 2 dc in same ch as first st of Row 1—opening for front leg formed; pc in center ch of foundation ch, 2 dc in next ch; ch 8, turn.
Row 28: Sk first ch, sc in each of 7 ch, 5 sc across center section, sc in next 7 ch, 25 sc across rem of row. Fasten off.

SECOND SIDE SECTION: *Row 29:* Join thread with sl st over ch 3 at beg of Row 8. Ch 3, make dc in same sp, work along side same as Row 21.
Rows 30–34: Rep rows 22–26.
Row 35: Rep Row 23.
Row 36: Work 25 sc across Row 35, sl st in first sc at beg of Row 28—opening for opposite front leg formed. Turn, sl st in last sc just made.

BODY: *Rnd 37:* Ch 3, 2 dc in same pl as sl st, (sk sc, pc in next sc, sk sc, 3 dc in next sc) 6 times; ch 5, 3 dc in last sc at end of Row 28—opening made for head; (sk sc, pc in next sc, sk sc, 3 dc in next sc) 10 times; sk sc, pc in next sc, sl st in top of ch-3 at beg of rnd—76 sts.

KNITTING & CROCHET ABBREVIATIONS

beg .... begin(ning)	k .... knit	sp .... space
bl.................................block	lp(s) .... loop(s)	st(s) ....stitch(es)
ch .... chain	p.................................purl	st st................stockinette stitch
cl .... cluster	pat .... pattern	tog.......................... together
dc ....double crochet	psso .... pass sl st over	trc.................... treble crochet
dec .... decrease	rem...................remaining	yo ....yarn over
dp.................double-pointed	rep...................repeat	* ...... repeat from * as indicated
dtr ....double treble	rnd ....round	( ) ....repeat between ( ) as
grp ....group	sc .... single crochet	indicated
hdc .... half-double crochet	sk ....skip	[ ]............. repeat between [ ] as
inc .... increase	sl st ....slip stitch	indicated

Rnd 38: Sl st in next dc, ch 1, sc in same place. Make sc in each dc, pc, and ch around, ending with sc in top of turning-ch at beg of Rnd 37; sl st in first sc made.

Rnd 39: **Ch 3, 4 dc in same place as sl st, drop lp from hook, insert hook in top of ch 3 and pull lp through—beg pc made;** (sk sc, 3 dc in next sc, sk sc, pc in next sc) 18 times, sk dc, 3 dc in next sc, sl st in first pc.

Rnd 40: Ch 1, sc in same st as last sc; sc in each st around; join with sl st in first sc of rnd.

Rnd 41: Ch 3, 2 dc in same place as sl st, (sk sc, pc in next sc, sk sc, 3 dc in next sc) 18 times, sk sc, pc in next sc, sl st in top of ch 3.

Rnd 42: Sl st in next dc, ch 1, sc in same st as last sl st; sc in each rem st around. Join with sl st in first sc.

Rnds 43–46: Rep rnds 39–42.

Rnd 47: Sl st in next 2 sc, ch 3, dc in sc where last sl st was just made. (Sk sc, pc in next sc, sk sc, 3 dc in next sc) 13 times; sk sc, pc in next sc, sk sc, 2 dc in next sc—57 sts. Ch 1, turn—rem 19 sc are used later for back leg openings and bottom of rear body section.

Row 48: Sc in each dc and pc across and in top of ch 3; ch 3, turn.

Row 49: Sk first 2 sc, (3 dc in next sc, sk sc, pc in next sc, sk sc) 13 times, 3 dc in next sc, sk sc, dc in last sc; ch 1, turn.

Row 50: Sc each st across; ch 3, turn.

Row 51: Dc in first sc, sk sc, pc in next sc, work across in usual pat, end with 2 dc in last sc; ch 1, turn.

Rows 52 and 53: Rep rows 48 and 49, omitting ch 1 at end of Row 53. Fasten off.

HEAD: *Rnd 1:* With wrong sides facing, join yarn with sl st in side of Row 25 at neck edge. Ch 3, complete beg pc in same place as sl st. Work around back of neck alternating 3-dc groups and pc evenly spaced so as to have a total of five 3-dc groups and 6 pc. Sixth pc is opposite side of neck in sp corresponding to beg pc. Dc over side sc of row directly after last pc, 2 dc over side dc of next row, 1 dc over side of next row, 2 dc over side dc of next row, dc in each dc and pc across 12 sts of front section, 7 dc over rem side rows. Join with sl st in top of first pc—total 25 dc around front for face.

Rnd 2: Ch 3, dc in same place as joining, (sk dc, pc in next dc, 3 dc in next pc) 4 times, pc in next dc, 2 dc in last pc, dc in 25 dc, sl st in top of ch-3.

Rnd 3: Ch 3, make beg pc in joining, (3 dc in next pc, sk dc, pc in next dc) 4 times; 3 dc in next pc, sk dc, pc in next dc, dc in next 10 dc, (2 dc in next dc, 1 dc in next dc) twice; 2 dc in next dc, dc in last 10 dc, sl st in top of ch-3.

Rnds 4–7: Rep rnds 2 and 3 twice, working 28 dc across face on each rnd.

Rnd 8: Work across back of head as in Rnd 2, dc in 10 dc, **(holding back on hook last lp of each st, make dc in next 2 dc, yo and draw through all lps on hook—dc dec made)** 4 times, dc in last 10 dc, join.

Rnd 9: Work back of head as in Rnd 3, dc in 9 dc, dc dec 3 times, dc in last 9 dc, join.

Rnd 10: Work back of head as Rnd 2, dc in 21 dc across face, join.

Rnd 11: Work back of head as Rnd 3, (sk dc, dc in next dc, sk dc, pc in next dc) twice, sk dc, dc in next dc, pc in center st, dc in next dc, (sk dc, pc in next dc, sk dc, dc in next dc) twice—32 sts. Join in top of first pc.

Rnd 12: Ch 3, (sk dc, pc in center dc, dc in next pc) 5 times, (pc in next dc, dc in next pc) 5 times, pc in last dc. Join in top of ch-3.

Rnd 13: Ch 3, making beg pc in same place as joining. (Dc in next pc, pc in next dc) 10 times, dc in last pc; join in top of first pc made.

Rnd 14: Sl st in next dc, ch 3, make beg pc in same place; (pc in next dc) 10 times. Join in top of first pc. Fasten off at end of Rnd 14, leaving 10 inches of yarn. Turn head inside out. Thread yarn into needle, weave through top of the 11 pc sts. Draw up tightly; tie off.

FRONT LEG: *Rnd 1:* With right sides facing, join yarn with sl st in any place along either leg opening. Ch 3, make beg pc in same place as sl st. Work around edge, alternating 3-dc groups and pc evenly spaced to make six of each. Join with sl st in top of first pc.

Rnd 2: Ch 1, sc in joining, sc in each dc and pc around, join—24 sts.

Rnd 3: Ch 3, 2 dc in first sc, (sk sc, pc in next sc, sk sc, 3 dc in next sc) 5 times, sk sc, pc in sc, sl st in top of ch-3.

Rnd 4: Sl st in next dc, ch 1, make 24 sc around, join.

Rnd 5: Ch 3, make beg pc in same place as sl st, continue in pat around, join.

Rnds 6–11: Rep rnds 2–5, then rep rnds 2 and 3 once more. Fasten off.

continued

HOOF: *Rnd 1:* Join black yarn with sl st in any st on lower edge of leg. Ch 3, (dc-dec, dc in next st) 7 times, dc-dec, join in top of ch-3—16 sts.

Rnd 2: Ch 3, dc in next dc, dc dec 7 times, sl st in top of first dc made—9 sts. Fasten off black, leaving 10 inches of yarn. Turn leg inside out. Thread yarn into needle, weave through top of 8 dc, draw up tightly and fasten off. Rep for other front leg.

REAR BODY SECTION: *Row 1:* Right side facing, sk first 7 sc of 19 sc of Rnd 47 that rem free for leg openings and rear body. Join yarn in eighth sc, ch 3, dc in same place. Sk sc, pc in sc, sk sc, 2 dc in next sc, ch 1, turn—7 sc left on each side for leg opening.

Row 2: Work 5 sc across; ch 3, turn.

Row 3: Dc in first sc, sk sc, pc in sc, sk sc, 2 dc in last sc; ch 1, turn.

Rows 4–6: Rep rows 2 and 3, then rep Row 2 once more.

Row 7: Make 2 dc in first sc, sk sc, pc in next sc, sk sc, 3 dc in last sc—7 sts; ch 1, turn.

Row 8: Sc in each st across; ch 3, turn.

Row 9: Dc in first sc, pc in second sc, sk sc, 3 dc in next sc, sk sc, pc in next sc, 2 dc in last sc—9 sts; ch 1, turn.

Row 10: Rep Row 8.

Row 11: Sk first 2 sc, 3 dc in next sc, sk sc, pc in next sc, sk sc, 3 dc in next sc, sk sc, dc in last sc; ch 1, turn.

Row 12: Rep Row 8.

Row 13: Dc in first sc, sk sc, pc in sc, sk sc, 3 dc in next sc, sk sc, pc in next sc, sk sc, 2 dc in last sc; ch 1, turn.

Rows 14–27: Rep rows 10–13 three times, then work rows 10 and 11 once more. Fasten off at end of Row 27, leaving 15-inch length of yarn. Thread yarn into needle, sew edge of Row 27 to top center back of body section. Continue sewing rem edges together, ending with corner of body coming at side of Row 8 of back section. Sew opposite corner of body to Row 8 on other side of rear section. Sew upper edges together, leaving a 3- or 4-inch opening near top for stuffing.

BACK LEGS: Work each back leg and hoof as for Front Legs. Stuff lamb firmly and sew closed.

TAIL: Leaving 15-inch length of yarn at beginning, ch 24. Join with sl st to form ring.

Rnd 1: Ch 3, making beg pc in same ch as joining. (Sk ch, 3 dc in next ch, sk ch, pc in next ch) 5 times, sk ch, 3 dc in next ch, sl st in top of first pc.

Rnd 2: Ch 3, 2 dc in same place as joining, (sk dc, pc in next dc, 3 dc in next pc) 5 times, sk dc, pc in next dc. Join in top of ch-3.

Rnd 3: Sl st in next dc, ch 3, make beg pc in same place, (3 dc in next pc, sk dc, pc in next dc) 5 times, 3 dc in last pc. Join in top of first pc.

Rnd 4: Rep Rnd 2.

Rnd 5: Sl st in next dc, ch 3, make beg pc in same place, (dc in next pc, sk dc, pc in next dc) 5 times, dc in last pc. Join in top of first pc.

Rnd 6: Sl st in next dc, ch 3, make beg pc in same place, (pc in next dc) 5 times. Join in first pc. Fasten off, leaving 10 inches of yarn. Thread yarn into needle. With tail inside out, weave yarn through top of 6 pc, draw up tightly; tie off. Turn tail right side out, stuff firmly. Thread yarn end from beg of first row of tail into needle. Sew tail to back of body at top of rear section.

NOSE: With black, ch 5, sl st to form ring.

Rnd 1: Ch 3, make 11 dc in ring, join in top of ch-3.

Rnd 2: Ch 3, dc in same place as sl st, (dc in next dc, 2 dc in next dc) 5 times, dc in last dc. Join in top of ch-3—18 sts. Fasten off, leaving 15-inch length of yarn. Thread yarn into needle. Sew nose to center of face, stuffing nose firmly with black yarn clippings before opening is closed.

EYE: Use needle and yarn to embroider several vertical satin or buttonhole stitches for each eye.

EAR: (Make 2) With white, ch 4.

Row 1: Work 2 dc in fourth ch from hook—3 sts; ch 3, turn.

Row 2: Dc in next 2 dc, 2 dc in top of ch-3—5 sts; ch 3, turn.

Row 3: Dc in first dc, dc in next 3 dc, 2 dc in top of ch-3—7 sts; ch 3, turn.

Row 4: Dc in second dc, dc in next 4 dc, dc in top of ch-3; ch 3, turn.

Row 5: Dc in first dc, dc in next 5 dc, 2 dc in top of ch-3—9 sts; ch 3, turn.

Row 6: Dc in second dc, dc in next 6 dc, dc in top of ch-3; ch 3, turn.

Row 7: Dc dec over second and third dc, dc in next 3 dc, dc dec over last 2 dc, dc in top of ch-3—7 sts; ch 3, turn.

Row 8: Dc dec over second and third dc, dc in next dc, dc dec over last 2 dc, dc in top of ch-3—5 sts. Fasten off, leaving 10-inch length of yarn. Sew ear to side of head at top of face section.

Stocking Bear

Shown on page 24.
Finished bear is 10 inches tall.

MATERIALS

One pair of men's terry crew socks
Two 12-millimeter plastic eyes
1¾-inch-diameter piece plastic canvas
Black embroidery floss
Polyester fiberfill
2x24-inch strip of fabric (bow)
Dressmaker's carbon paper, pencil
Graph paper

INSTRUCTIONS

Enlarge the pattern, *below,* onto graph paper. Turn the terry side of the socks to the inside. Using carbon paper, transfer stitching lines onto the socks.

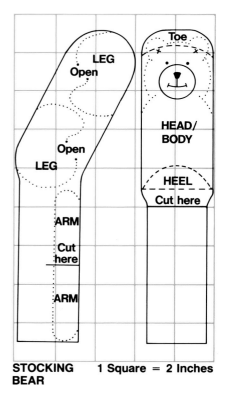

STOCKING BEAR   1 Square = 2 Inches

Machine-stitch through both layers of each sock along marked lines, leaving the openings and sock bottoms unstitched. Cut out the body parts; trim the seams.

MUZZLE: Cut a ½-inch-diameter hole in the center of the plastic canvas circle. Working on the smooth side of the sock, hand-stitch the perimeter of the circle in place on bear's face.

Push fiberfill through the center hole in the plastic canvas to create a smooth round muzzle.

HEAD/BODY: Turn the head/body right side out. Sew on eyes. Stuff the head/body, gradually increasing the circumference to 11 inches at the bottom. Sew the openings closed.

Tack the ears front to back at the head line. Using six strands of floss, straight-stitch a mouth and satin-stitch the nose.

Tie a bow around bear's neck using fabric strip; trim fabric ends.

LEGS: Turn legs right side out. Stuff each leg to measure 5 inches long, 7½ inches around the thigh, and 4 inches around the foot. Sew openings closed. Hand-sew the legs to the body.

ARMS: Turn the arms right side out. Stuff each arm to measure 4 inches long and 4 inches in circumference. Fold the excess length back into the arms. Hand-sew the arms to the body.

Knitted Teddy Bear

Shown on page 25.
Bear is 20 inches tall.

MATERIALS
Bartlettyarns Glen Tweed: two 4-oz. skeins of bronze No. G-1010
Set of Size 9 double-pointed needles (dpn) or size to reach gauge given
Size H crochet hook
Tapestry needle
Black wool felt scraps
Polyester fiberfill

Abbreviations: See page 35.
Gauge: Over st st, 4 sts = 1 inch.

INSTRUCTIONS
Note: The bear is made in one piece.
HEAD: Beg at back of head, with H hook, ch 4; join with sl st to form ring and work 8 sc into ring.

Rnd 1: With dpn, pick up 1 st in front lp and 1 st in back lp of each st around—16 sts.
Rnd 2: Work even.
Rnd 3: Inc 8 sts evenly spaced—24 sts.
Rnd 4: Work even.
Rnd 5: Rep Rnd 3—32 sts.
Rnd 6: Work even.
Rnd 7: Rep Rnd 3—40 sts.
Work even for 14 rnds. Stuff the head firmly.

SNOUT: Dec 8 sts evenly spaced—32 sts; work even 3 rnds. Dec 6 sts evenly spaced—26 sts. Work even 5 rnds. Dec 5 sts evenly spaced—21 sts. Work even 5 rnds. Dec 3 sts evenly spaced—18 sts. Work even 1 rnd. K 2 tog around—9 sts; stuff snout firmly. Work even 1 rnd.

Fasten off, leaving 4-inch tail; thread yarn onto needle, run needle through sts, removing dpn. Gather and darn closed, burying yarn end in stuffing.

NECK: Referring to the diagram, *below right,* pick up 25 sts in circle at base of head. Work even 1 rnd.

BODY: Inc in each st around—50 sts. Work even 24 rnds, marking center back of body. Stuff body until firm.

SEAT: To shape seat, work short rows as follows. *Next rnd:* Work 12 sts beyond center back marker, turn; p 24 sts, turn.

Next row: Sl 1, k 1, psso, k to within last 2 seat sts, k 2 tog; turn—22 sts.

Following row: P seat sts. Rep these last 2 rows until 12 sts rem, ending with wrong-side row.

Next row: Work around entire piece, picking up 7 sts along each shaped edge of seat—50 sts. Work even 1 rnd.

LEG: Sl first 25 sts to holder (center back to center front). Work rem 25 sts in the round for 24 rnds.

HEEL: Turn as for seat, beg with 9 sts at center back of leg and dec to 3 sts, ending with a wrong-side row.

FOOT: Work a complete rnd, picking up 3 sts along each shaped edge of heel—25 sts. Work even 5 rnds. Dec 5 sts evenly spaced—20 sts; work even 4 rnds. Dec 4 sts evenly spaced—16 sts; work 2 rnds even. K 2 tog around—8 sts; work even 1 rnd. Stuff leg and foot; close toe as for head.

ARMS: Mark 10 sts on first work-even rnd after neck shaping (refer to diagram, *below*). Pick up 10 sts; turn. Pick up 10 sts on next rnd below—20 sts. Work even 1 rnd. Inc 4 sts evenly spaced—24 sts. Work 24 rnds even. Stuff arm.

WRIST: Dec to 12 sts; work even 1 rnd. Inc to 24 sts; work even 5 rnds. Dec to 12 sts, work even 1 rnd. Stuff arm and paw. Close as for head.

EARS: Referring to diagram, *below,* pick up 8 sts. Turn, p back. Dec 1 st at each end of next row—6 sts. Bind off. Join yarn at left side of ear; with crochet hook, work 1 row reverse sc along entire edge of ear. Make second ear.

EYES, NOSE, FOOT PADS, AND TOES: Using photograph on page 25 as guide for shape and placement, sew black wool felt shapes in place using black thread. Highlight eyes with white thread.

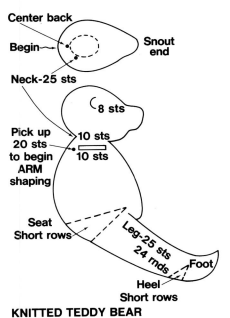

KNITTED TEDDY BEAR

Holiday Workshop

Christmas is a fantasy time for children, with a treat at every turn. Designed with kids in mind, these cross-stitched ornaments will help everyone share the holiday spirit.

The six familiar shapes used for these fun perforated paper cross-stitch decorations are easy for youngsters to identify. And, because the stitching is so quick and easy, a set of ornaments can be the ideal gift for teachers and school friends.

Much of the shape is left unstitched, so you can make the whole batch in a twinkling. Finishing chores are cut to a minimum by just trimming excess paper.

Basic primary colors of floss and small pieces of perforated paper are all you need for each ornament. The finished pieces, hung with ribbon or thread, can deck a tree, trim a gift package, or decorate a holiday wreath. Or, use the designs to personalize special note cards by mounting the stitched perforated paper on colored card paper.

Finished sizes range from 2½x3½ inches to 5x5½ inches.

Directions and stitching charts follow on pages 40 and 41.

Cross-Stitched Paper Ornaments

Shown on pages 38 and 39.

MATERIALS
White or ecru perforated paper
Embroidery floss in the following colors: black, white, purple, pink, orange, red, gold, yellow, brown, green, light blue, blue, dark blue
Tapestry needle
Felt or colored card stock (optional)

INSTRUCTIONS
Referring to the stitch count on each chart, cut pieces of perforated paper to the appropriate size for each design, allowing an extra inch all around. Beginning at the top of a design, work cross-stitches over one square of paper using two plies of floss.

To prevent floss from snagging on the cut edges, fold narrow masking tape over the edges.

Perforated paper has a right and a wrong side; the wrong side is rougher to the touch. Any necessary markings can be made lightly in pencil on the wrong side.

All backstitches are indicated in red, green, or black. On the Christmas Tree design, outline the packages with dark blue backstitches and the bear with brown backstitches.

FINISHING: When the stitching is complete, carefully trim excess paper, leaving a margin equivalent to one row of stitching around each design.

To make a tree ornament, glue the stitched paper onto felt or colored card stock to conceal the back, if desired. Cut colored backing close to the edge of the paper. For a hanger, run a length of thread through the paper backing.

Stitching on Perforated Paper

Handle perforated paper with care. Like all paper, it is damaged when folded or bent. To prevent tearing it as you work, tape or staple the edges to a frame. And, because the paper cannot be washed, work with clean, dry hands.

As you stitch, maintain a light tension to prevent tearing the paper. Never carry floss behind unstitched areas because it will show through the holes.

Perforated paper is widely available in 14-count white, ecru, and antique brown.

Stitch Count 52x75

COLOR KEY
⊠ Red
⊠ Green
◎ Yellow
⊡ White
▣ Black

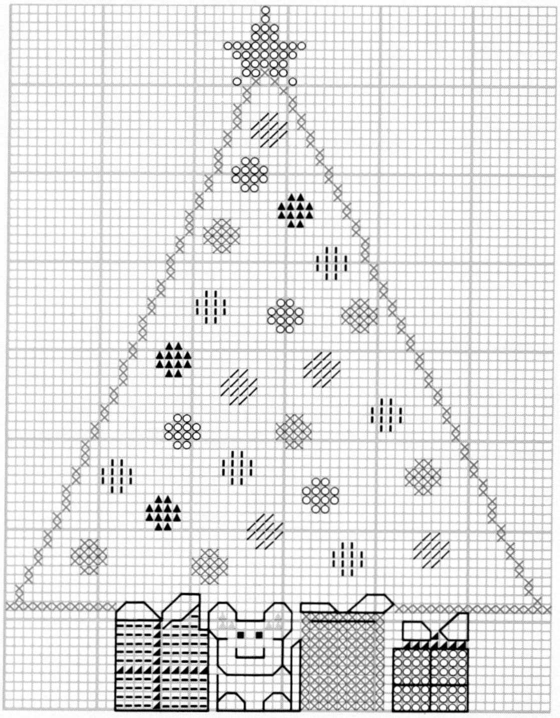

Stitch Count 59x79

COLOR KEY
⊠ Green
Pink
▣ Black
⊟ Light Blue
◪ Dark Blue
◎ Yellow
⊠ Red
▲ Purple
◺ Blue
Ⅰ Orange

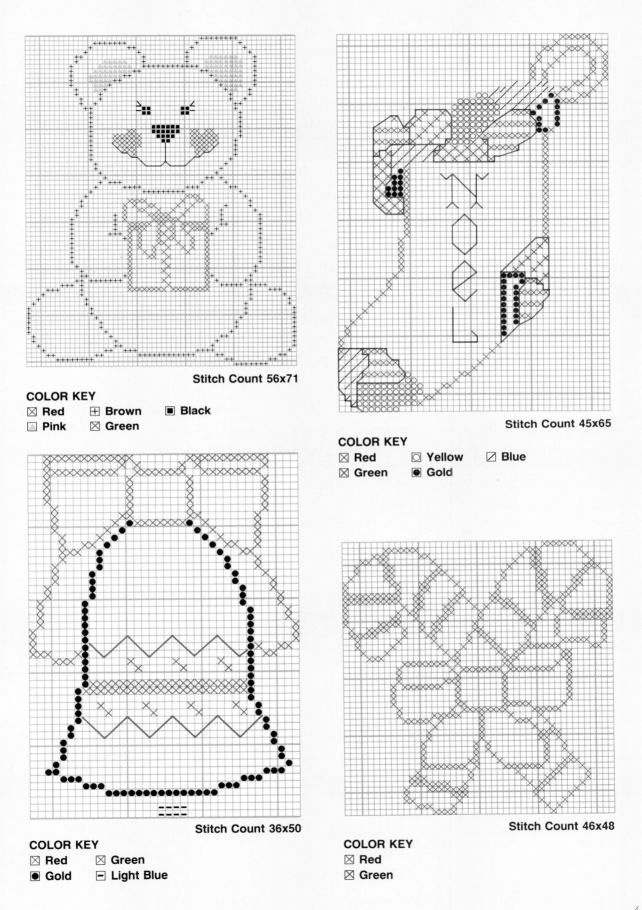

Stitch Count 56x71

COLOR KEY

⊠ Red	⊞ Brown	▣ Black
◩ Pink	⊠ Green	

Stitch Count 45x65

COLOR KEY

⊠ Red	○ Yellow	⊘ Blue
⊠ Green	◉ Gold	

Stitch Count 36x50

COLOR KEY

⊠ Red	⊠ Green
◉ Gold	⊟ Light Blue

Stitch Count 46x48

COLOR KEY

⊠ Red
⊠ Green

Christmas at Grandma's

Memories of childhood Christmases at Grandma's warm the hearts of far-flung families who come together to celebrate the season. Homemade holiday treats carry us back to those times and build new memories for today's grandchildren.

Tea parties are among the treasured traditions at Grandma's house. Old-fashioned teacups and gingerbread teapot cookies decorated her tree, and she always baked plenty of extra cookies for the party.

The following pages feature crafts projects reminiscent of Grandma and her beloved teacups. Teapot pillows, snuggly afghans and quilts, and cuddly grandparent dolls recall the cozy comfort of the old home place.

Christmas morning is always filled with excitement and wonder. Underneath the tree are gifts lovingly crafted or purchased for each family member.

An embroidered teapot pillow, *left,* is a year-round reminder of Grandma's parties. Two shades of blue floss duplicate the patterns of old china in simple stitches on this 14x19-inch pillow.

For Christmas teas, Grandma serves in style with her prized tray, *below left.* A filet crochet tea set doily is displayed in a glass-covered wooden tray. Brightly colored fabric under the crochet highlights the 11½x18-inch design, made with only one ball of crochet cotton and basic crochet stitches.

Bright red strawberry ornaments add a warm glow to the shimmering tree, *opposite.* Gold beads pit the surface of the berry to make each 3½-inch-tall ornament a delight to stitch.

Scraps of fabric, trims, wool, and cardboard are all you need to create cuddly grandparent surrogates like those *opposite.* Standing 22 to 24 inches tall, both doll bodies are made of soft, durable felt.

Project instructions begin on page 51.

Newly crafted treasures take their places among the family favorites each year and bring joy to the holiday festivities.

The knitted houndstooth check and geese stocking, *left,* not only holds a feast of Christmas goodies, but also will become a cherished memento of Christmas. Measuring 22 inches long, it's knitted in sturdy rows of stockinette stitches on circular needles.

The cozy afghan's parade of waddling Christmas geese, *opposite,* copies the stocking's motifs in rows of stockinette stitches bordered with a garter-stitched edging. Tweedy yarns in rich tones of barn red, forest green, and creamy beige dramatize the country theme of this 48x60-inch knee warmer. Rows of the knitting are worked on circular needles to hold all the stitches.

Use the charted geese design on other needlework projects. For example, you can use duplicate stitches to work a gaggle of geese on a purchased sweater or scarf. Cross-stitchers will enjoy a gander or two on decorative towels or curtains.

Instructions for the stocking and afghan are on pages 56 and 57.

The magic of Christmas morning spreads throughout the day as everyone enjoys new toys and gifts. The simple traditions, presents crafted with love, and kindred spirits are as special as the moments spent curled up on Grandma's lap.

A warm knitted afghan, *opposite,* melts the children's cold toes while they cuddle and listen to Grandma's Christmas Eve stories. The big country plaid is knit on circular needles in stockinette stitch with tones of oatmeal, raspberry, and just a touch of Christmas teal green. Vertical rows of teal are worked in duplicate stitch. Luxurious fringe finishes off the 50x67-inch piece.

Simple Christmas-colored stripes sew together fast and easy for this festive holiday quilt, *above.* Quick cutting and piecing techniques even make the zigzag border a snap to assemble. As a special bonus, this quilt includes instructions for finishing the bottom corners with a cutout footboard allowance.

Illustrated directions for the quilt and afghan are on pages 57–59.

FULL-SIZE PATTERN

TEAPOT COOKIE

Gingerbread Teapot Cookies

Shown on pages 42 and 43.
Cookies are approximately 4½x7 inches.

INGREDIENTS

4 cups all-purpose flour
1 teaspoon ground cinnamon
1 teaspoon ground ginger
½ teaspoon baking soda
1 cup margarine *or* butter
1 cup packed brown sugar
1 egg
⅓ cup honey
1 teaspoon *finely* shredded lemon peel
2 tablespoons lemon juice
1 recipe Royal Icing (see recipe, *opposite*)

INSTRUCTIONS

In a medium mixing bowl stir together flour, cinnamon, ginger, and baking soda. Set aside.

Beat margarine with an electric mixer on medium speed for 30 seconds. Add brown sugar and beat till fluffy. Add egg, honey, lemon peel, and lemon juice; beat well. Gradually beat in flour mixture, stirring in the last part with a wooden spoon.

Divide the dough in half. Cover and chill the dough about 1 hour or until dough is no longer sticky. (If using corn oil margarine, cover and chill in freezer several hours.)

Trace the pattern, *left,* onto cardboard; cut out.

On a floured surface, roll the dough ¼ inch thick. Lay the teapot pattern on the dough; using a sharp knife, cut the dough into teapot shapes. Using two spatulas, transfer the cutouts to ungreased cookie sheets. Smooth any rough edges with your finger. With the end of a straw or the tip of a paring knife, make a hole in the top of each cookie to thread ribbon for hanging.

Bake the cookies in a 375° oven for 8 to 10 minutes or until slightly browned. Cool for two minutes on the cookie sheets. Transfer the cookies to a wire rack; let cool completely.

TEATIME FILET CROCHET TRAY

1 Square = 1 Block

To decorate, pipe Royal Icing onto cookies in patterns resembling china or teapot designs.

Thread ribbon through hole in each cookie; tie to tree.

Makes 8–10 teapot cookies.

ROYAL ICING: In a large mixer bowl, combine three *egg whites;* one 16-ounce package *powdered sugar,* sifted (about 4¾ cups); 1 teaspoon *vanilla;* and ½ teaspoon *cream of tartar.* Add several drops of red or green food coloring, if desired.

Beat with a heavy-duty electric mixer on high speed for 7 to 10 minutes or until very stiff. Use the icing at once, covering icing in bowl with wet paper towels to prevent drying as you work.

Makes 3 cups.

Filet Crochet Doily
Shown on pages 42 and 44.
Doily measures approximately
11½x18 inches.

MATERIALS
One large ball of No. 30 crochet
 cotton
Size 12 crochet hook
Glass-topped tray to fit needlework

Abbreviations: See page 35.

INSTRUCTIONS
Chain 297.

Row 1: Dc in fourth ch from hook and in each ch across—295 dc, counting beg ch-3 as dc; ch 3; turn. *Note:* Count each beg ch-3 as first dc of row.

Row 2: Sk first dc, dc in each dc across, working last dc in top of turning ch-3—295 dc and 98 blocks (bls) made; ch 3, turn.

Row 3: Sk first dc, dc in each of next 9 dc—3 bls made; ch 2, sk 2 dc, dc in next dc—sp made; dc in each of next 3 dc to complete bl; (ch 2, sk 2 dc, dc in next dc) 7 times—7 sps made; in bl and sp pat established, work (1 bl, 2 sps, 1 bl, 6 sps) 7 times; then work 1 bl, 2 sps, 1 bl, 7 sps, 1 bl, 1 sp, ending with 3 bls; ch 3, turn.

Row 4: Referring to chart *above,* work in rows as established, working a bl for each darkened square on the chart and a sp for each vacant square on the chart. *Note:* Sk first dc of each row. Work rows of chart from right to left on odd-numbered rows and from left to right on even-numbered rows.

FINISHING: Block the completed stitchery. Purchase or build a wooden tray to fit the finished stitchery. Place fabric under the needlework to accentuate the design. Cover the needlework with glass for protection.

TEAPOT PILLOW

1 Square = 1 Inch

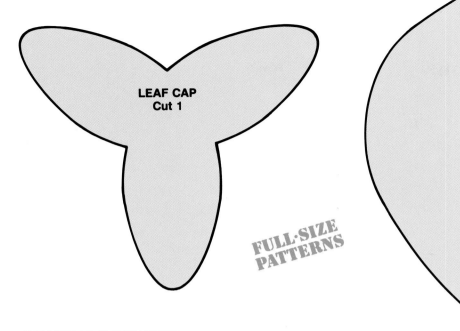

LEAF CAP
Cut 1

Top

STRAWBERRY
Cut 3

FULL-SIZE PATTERNS

STRAWBERRY ORNAMENT

Teapot Pillow

Shown on page 44.
Pillow measures 14x19 inches.

MATERIALS
Two 15x20-inch pieces of muslin
Purchased blue piping
One skein *each* of DMC embroidery
  floss in light blue (826) and dark
  blue (825)
Polyester fiberfill
Graph paper and pencil

INSTRUCTIONS
Enlarge pattern *opposite* onto graph paper. Transfer all lines and dots to one
piece of muslin. With three strands of
light blue floss, outline-stitch the birds,
scallops, and spout band. (Refer to
stitch diagrams on page 156.) Dots indicate French knots. Stitch remaining
lines with three strands of dark blue.

Draw a stitching line 1 inch beyond
teapot outline, gently shaping around
the curved areas. Cut out the pillow
front, adding ¼-inch seam allowances.
Cut a pillow back to match.

Baste piping to pillow front along
the drawn stitching line. With right
sides facing, stitch pillow front to back,
leaving an opening for turning. Clip
seam allowances at curves; turn and
stuff. Stitch the opening closed.

Strawberry Ornament

Shown on page 45.
Finished ornament is approximately
3½ inches high.

MATERIALS
4x12-inch piece of bright red
  velveteen
3x3-inch piece of green felt
9 inches of narrow green ribbon
Gold rocaille beads
Polyester fiberfill
Pinking shears
Cardboard or template plastic

INSTRUCTIONS
Trace the full-size patterns *above* onto
template material. *These patterns include*
¼-inch seam allowances. Cut three strawberry pieces from red velveteen. Using
pinking shears, cut one leaf cap from
green felt.

With right sides together, sew the
three strawberry pieces together, leaving an opening in one seam for turning. Clip seam allowances; turn berry
right side out and stuff firmly. Slip-
stitch the opening closed.

Tack a leaf cap to the strawberry top.

Randomly sew beads around berry
to simulate seeds. Attach ribbon loop
to top of ornament for hanging.

Grandparent Dolls

Shown on page 45.
Finished dolls are 22–24 inches tall.

MATERIALS
■ **For both dolls**
1 yard flesh-colored felt for bodies
2 pairs 1-inch teddy bear joints
Felt scraps in blue, white, and tan
20 inches ½-inch-wide elastic
Black pearl cotton
Transparent nylon thread
Two 6x8-inch scraps heavy cardboard
Two 6x8-inch scraps of lightweight
  black cardboard for slippers
Polyester fiberfill
Crafts glue
Powdered blush
Large needle or awl
Graph paper and pencil

■ **For Grandma doll**
1 yard wool roving for hair
⅜ yard fabric *each* for bloomers,
  apron, and dress
1 yard narrow lace trim
12 inches pregathered eyelet
14 inches narrow braid trim
2 gray felt squares for slippers
1 yard rickrack for slipper trim
Purchased ribbon rosette trim

continued

■ For Grandpa doll
¼ yard fake fur for Grandpa's hair
⅓ yard fabric *each* for pants, shirt,
  and sweater
3x16-inch piece of bow-tie fabric
3 small shirt buttons
2 black felt squares for slippers
½ yard braid for slipper trim

INSTRUCTIONS
Note: Patterns include ¼-inch seam allowances; sew all seams with right sides of fabrics facing.

Enlarge the patterns on pages 55 and 56 onto graph paper. Cut all pieces *except* face profiles, ears, and slipper soles from appropriate fabrics.

■ For both bodies
Sew body center front seam. With center dots matching, sew a foot to bottom of each front leg.

Sew body back to front, leaving openings as indicated. Sew a sole to each foot, sewing all the way around the circle formed by the joined foot and back leg; turn right side out. Stuff feet and legs through side openings; slip-stitch the opening closed. Working from the top opening, continue to add stuffing up to the waist area.

Sew arms together in pairs, leaving openings as indicated. Stuff hands. Hand-stitch between joined fingers.

At the shoulder dot, make a small hole on the *inside* of the arm with a large needle or awl. Insert half a joint inside the arm, pushing the point or cotter pin through the hole. Stuff the rest of the arm, keeping disk of joint flat against the felt. Slip-stitch opening closed; repeat for other arm.

On the body, make matching holes at the shoulder dots. Join arms to body through holes and secure with remaining joint parts, working on the inside of the body through the top opening. Stuff body; slip-stitch opening closed.

HEAD: Draw face profiles onto double thicknesses of felt. Stitch profiles on drawn lines; trim excess. Draw facial features on each profile. Using black pearl cotton, backstitch mouths, eye outlines, and Grandma's eyebrows.

For Grandma, cut blue felt eyes; glue or sew eyes inside outlines. Glue white felt accents to pupils. Brush cheeks with powdered blush.

For Grandpa, cut white felt rectangles for eyes; glue in place. Glue tan felt irises in center of white felt; hand-sew in place. Glue white felt accents to irises. Brush cheeks with blush.

With right sides up, open profile to lie flat; push nose to one side. Lay head back over face with center seams of profile matching center fold line of head back. Sew head back to profile, leaving opening at top for turning.

Stuff head, leaving nose unstuffed. Slip-stitch top opening closed.

Wrap the roving around Grandma's head, beginning at face and ending at the back, forming a bun shape. Sew in place with transparent thread.

Pin Grandpa's hair and sideburns in place so the ear opening falls at the head seam line. Glue hair in place, starting with sideburns and continuing around outer edges.

Draw the ear outline onto a double thickness of felt. Stitch on the curved line; trim excess. Turn to right side; slip-stitch opening closed. Machine-stitch the earlobe detail. Hand-sew ears onto head between sideburns and hair.

Cut small scraps of fake fur for eyebrows and a mustache; glue in place. Set heads aside.

■ Clothing and Assembly
DRESS: Stay-stitch across shoulder top as indicated by dotted line at armhole edge. Clip seam at shoulder top. Match dot on sleeve top to shoulder clip; sew sleeve to dress, pivoting at dot.

Sew side and underarm seams. Narrowly hem sleeves and lower dress edge. Slip dress on doll.

Position head on body top. Hand-sew back of head to top of body, sewing through clothing.

SHIRT: Sew shirt same as for dress. Slip shirt on doll; add Grandpa's head in the same manner as Grandma's.

Cut two 2x6-inch strips for cuffs. Fold in ½ inch on long sides and ¼ inch on ends; topstitch all edges. Pleat sleeve to fit wrist; tack to arm. Slip-stitch cuff to sleeve edge, overlapping cuff ends on outside edge of sleeve. Sew buttons down shirt front.

BLOOMERS: Sew center front and back seams. Sew inner leg seam. Fold under upper edge to make a casing; sew in place, leaving a small opening. Insert elastic through opening; slip-stitch opening closed. Narrowly hem each leg; trim edge with narrow lace.

TROUSERS: Sew in same manner as bloomers, sewing outer leg seams after center seams.

APRON: Hem all pocket edges. Baste braid around curved edge; sew pocket to apron, sewing through braid.

Sew lining to front, leaving openings as indicated. Turn and press. On front, sew braid ½ inch from neck edge between shoulder seams.

Cut two 2x20-inch waistline ties and two 1½x9-inch neckline ties. Narrowly hem ties, leaving one end unfinished. Slip raw ends of waistline ties into corner openings; slip raw ends of neckline ties into shoulder openings. Topstitch around all edges of the apron, stitching ties in place.

Turn ends of shoulder ties up 1 inch; sew across end to form loop. Put apron on, crisscross shoulder ties, and slip waist ties through loops. Tie at back.

SWEATER: Hem front, neck, and lower edges. Finish sweater in same manner as dress. Hem all the pocket edges; topstitch pockets on front.

Slip sweater on doll. Turn 1½ inches of sleeve edge to inside; blindstitch in place. Turn hemmed edge back to right side, forming cuff.

BOW TIE: Cut 3x14-inch strip for tie. Fold fabric in half lengthwise; sew
continued

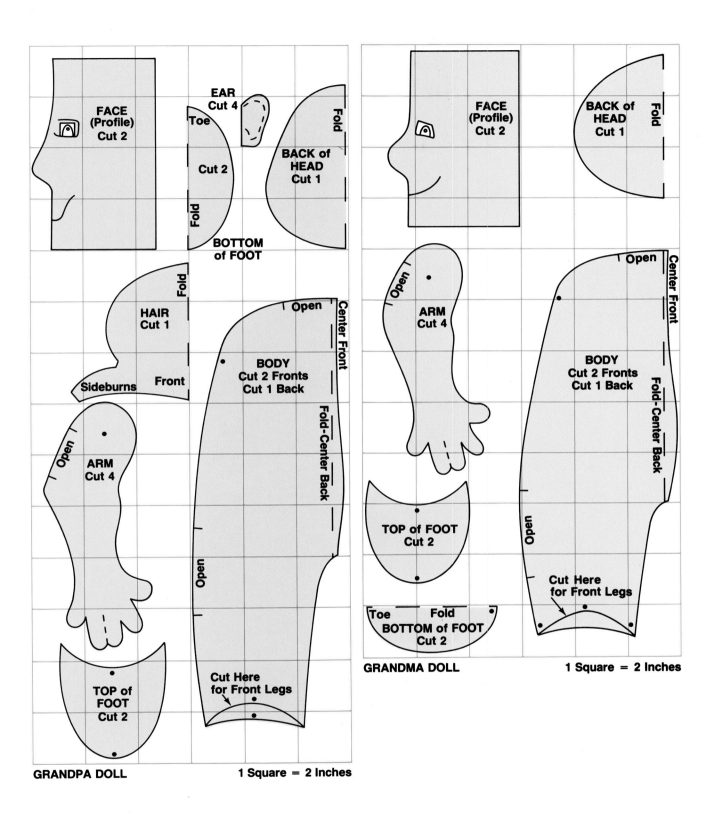

FACE
(Profile)
Cut 2

EAR
Cut 4

Toe

Cut 2

Fold

BOTTOM
of FOOT

Fold

BACK of
HEAD
Cut 1

Fold

HAIR
Cut 1

Sideburns

Front

Open

Center Front

BODY
Cut 2 Fronts
Cut 1 Back

Fold-Center Back

Open

ARM
Cut 4

Open

TOP of
FOOT
Cut 2

Cut Here
for Front Legs

GRANDPA DOLL

1 Square = 2 Inches

FACE
(Profile)
Cut 2

BACK of
HEAD
Cut 1

Fold

Open

ARM
Cut 4

Open

Center Front

BODY
Cut 2 Fronts
Cut 1 Back

Fold-Center Back

Open

TOP of FOOT
Cut 2

Toe   Fold
BOTTOM of FOOT
Cut 2

Cut Here
for Front Legs

GRANDMA DOLL

1 Square = 2 Inches

across ends and long edge, leaving opening for turning. Turn to right side; slip-stitch opening closed.

Fold in bow-tie fashion. Cut a 2x2½-inch strip from same fabric. Fold the strip in half lengthwise and sew it in the same manner as for the tie. Wrap narrow strip around center of bow tie; slip-stitch ends together in back.

SLIPPERS: Cut the slipper soles from heavy and lightweight cardboard. Cut felt soles ¼ inch larger all around than cardboard. Glue felt to heavy cardboard sole; fold excess felt over and glue to bottom. Glue lightweight black sole over slipper bottom.

Slip-stitch slipper top to edge of sole. Glue rickrack or braid along edges of top. Glue ribbon rosettes in place.

Christmas Goose Stocking

Shown on page 46.
Finished stocking measures 22 inches long.

MATERIALS

Tahki Imports Designer Homespun Tweed (100-gram skein): one skein *each* of green (213) and beige (222)
Tahki Imports Donegal Tweed: one skein of red (817)
Size 8 circular needle (16-inch length)
Set of Size 8 double-pointed needles
Size G crochet hook
2 stitch holders
Tapestry needle

Abbreviations: See page 35.
Gauge: Over st st following Chart 2, 9 sts = 2 inches.

INSTRUCTIONS

Note on two-color knitting: When changing yarn colors, always twist the new color around the color in use to avoid making holes. Carry the unused color loosely across back, twisting it every three or four stitches.

TOP: Beg at top with circular needle and beige, cast on 68 sts. Join, being careful not to twist sts; place marker for beg of rnd. K 6 beige rnds, p 1 beige rnd, k 2 red rnds, k 1 beige rnd, p 1 beige rnd, k 3 green rnds. Continuing to k all rnds, work Chart 1, *opposite top,* upside down, repeating bet letters C and B of chart. When 20 rnds of Chart 1 are completed, k 4 green rnds, k 1 beige rnd, p 1 beige rnd, k 2 red rnds, k 1 beige rnd, p 1 beige rnd. Begin to follow Chart 2, *opposite above,* and k all rnds.

Keep to pat and at the same time, dec 1 st each side of marker every 1½ inches 4 times—60 sts. Fasten off.

Sl 15 sts each side of marker to one dpn, divide rem 30 sts on 2 holders.

HEEL: Change to beige yarn and work only on 30 sts that are on the one dpn.
Row 1: With wrong side facing, p 30, turn.
Row 2: Sl 1, k 29.
Row 3: Sl 1, p 29. Rep rows 2 and 3 until you have total of 18 rows.

TURN HEEL: *Row 1:* (wrong side) P 17, p 2 tog, p 1, turn.
Row 2: Sl 1, k 5, k 2 tog, k 1, turn. Keeping to st st work as follows:
Row 3: Sl 1, work to within 1 st of hole made by slipped st on previous row, work 2 tog, work 1 st, turn. Rep this row until all sts are worked—18 sts rem. Fasten off.

FOOT: Sl 9 sts back to right needle. With right side facing, and following Chart 2, beg on next row so as to keep color pat constant as established on instep sts.

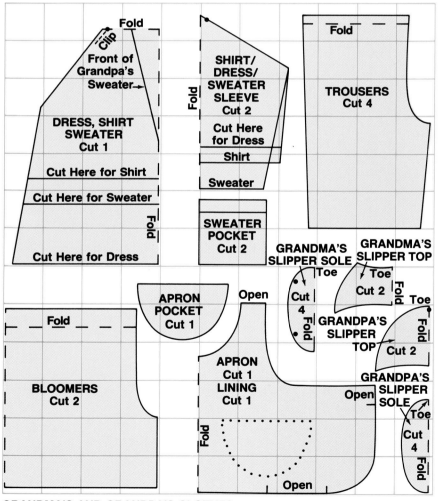

GRANDMA'S AND GRANDPA'S CLOTHES

1 Square = 2 Inches

Rnd 1: Place marker for beg of rnd, k 9 sts from center of heel to corner, pick up and k 10 sts along side of heel, k across 30 instep sts from holders, pick up and k 10 sts on side of heel, work rem 9 sts from heel—68 sts.

Rnd 2: K 17, k 2 tog with green, place second marker, k 30, place third marker; with green sl 1, k 1, psso, k 17.

Rnd 3: Knit.

Rnd 4: Keeping to pat, k to within 2 sts of the second marker, k 2 tog with green, sl marker, k 30, sl marker; with green sl 1, k 1, psso; complete rnd—64 sts. Rep these last 2 rnds, dec 1 st before second marker and after third marker every other rnd using green and keeping to color pat until 44 sts rem and changing to dpn as number of sts requires. Remove second and third markers, work even following Chart 2 until 7 inches from heel.

SHAPE TOE: Change to beige and dpn. *Rnd 1:* K 8, k 2 tog, k 2, sl 1, k 1, psso, k 16, k 2 tog, k 2, sl 1, k 1, psso, k 8—40 sts.

Rnd 2: Knit.

Rnd 3: K 7, k 2 tog, k 2, sl 1, k 1, psso, k 14, k 2 tog, k 2, sl 1, k 1, psso, k 7—36 sts. Rep rnds 2 and 3 until only 16 sts rem. Close the toe with Kitchener st, *below.*

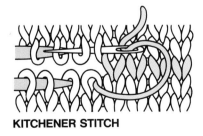

KITCHENER STITCH

FINISHING: Fold the top of the stocking to the inside along the first purl ridge and slip-stitch in place. Weave in all ends. With crochet hook and double strand of beige, work 10-st chain; attach at top back of stocking.

CHART 1

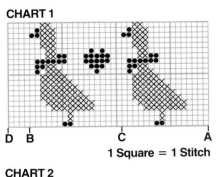

1 Square = 1 Stitch

CHART 2

☐ Green   ☒ Beige   ⬤ Red

GOOSE AFGHAN AND STOCKING

Christmas Goose Afghan

Shown on page 47.
Finished afghan is 48x60 inches.

MATERIALS

Tahki Imports Designer Homespun Tweed (100-gram skein): seven skeins of green (213); one skein of beige (222)
Tahki Imports Donegal Tweed (100-gram skein): six skeins of red (817)
Sizes 6 and 8 circular needles (29-inch length)

Abbreviations: See page 35.
Gauge: In st st over Chart 2, 9 sts = 2 inches.

INSTRUCTIONS

Note: The afghan is worked back and forth in rows on circular needles.

Note on two-color knitting: When changing yarn colors, always twist the new color around the color in use to avoid making holes. Carry the unused color loosely across the back, twisting it every three or four stitches.

With the smaller needle and red yarn, cast on 217 sts. Work even in garter st (knit every row) for 8 rows.

Change to larger needle, and keeping first 5 sts and last 5 sts of every row in garter st and red, work center 207 sts as follows: Work 8 rows in st st with green, *** work 2 rows garter st with beige, 2 rows st st with red, 2 rows garter st with beige.*** Continue with

st st over center 207 sts as follows: 4 rows green; beg Chart 1, *left,* working from A to B, then rep bet C and B 10 times, ending last rep at D. Follow the chart as established until all 20 rows are completed. Work 4 rows green, rep bet *s once, inc 1 st over center 207 sts in last row—218 sts.

Keeping first 5 sts and last 5 sts in garter st with red as before, continue over center 208 sts in st st following Chart 2, *left,* until total length measures approximately 51½ inches, ending with Row 4 of Chart 2.

Rep bet *s once, dec 1 st over center 208 sts in first row—217 sts. Work 4 rows in st st with green; continuing in st st, follow Chart 1, working from top to bottom to reverse motifs; work 4 rows in st st with green, rep bet *s once, work 8 rows in st st with green.

Change to smaller needles; work in garter st over all 217 sts for 8 rows with red. Bind off.

Weave in all ends. Block lightly with damp cloth and warm iron.

Stripe Quilt

Shown on page 49.
Quilt measures 89 inches square.

MATERIALS

5 yards of white or muslin fabric
3½ yards of red print fabric
2⅓ yards of green print fabric
5¼ yards of backing fabric
Quilt batting
Rotary cutter and cutting mat
Heavy-duty plastic ruler

INSTRUCTIONS

Note: Measurements given include ¼-inch seam allowances. Cutting requirements state the exact length needed; you may want to cut the strips longer to allow for error, then trim the strips to the correct length as you sew. Cutting the strips longer also will enable you to make the quilt longer to fit your bed, if desired.

CUTTING: First cut strips for the main section of the quilt, then cut border strips. Keep border strips separate.

From the white fabric, cut an 81-inch length. From this piece, cut five strips 5½x80½ inches and eight strips

continued

1¾x80½ inches. Next, cut four 3-inch-wide strips across the width of the fabric. Use these to piece two strips each 3x69¼ inches. From remaining white fabric, cut four strips 1¾x69¼ inches and one strip 1¾x53 inches.

For the border, cut two white strips 2x69¼ inches, 10 strips 1¾x72 inches, and 10 strips 1x72 inches.

For the red quilt strips, cut eight 1¾x80½ inches, two 1¾x86¾ inches, and two 1¾x69¼ inches. For the border, cut 10 red strips 1½x72 inches.

From the green fabric, cut four strips 1¾x80½ inches, two strips 1¾x69¼ inches, and one 1¾x53 inches. For the border, cut four green strips 1¾x69¼ inches and five strips 1½x72 inches.

ZIGZAG BORDER UNITS: Join seven strips into the strip set illustrated in Figure 1, *top right.* Make five 72-inch-long strip sets.

Cut each strip set into segments for zigzags. Cut 30 *each* of segment A and segment B as shown in Figure 2, *above right.* To cut segments, mark 5-inch increments on the bottom white strip. Make a 45-degree cut at each mark.

Combine A and B segments as shown in Figure 3, *above, far right.* Then trim each zigzag unit to 6¾ inches wide by 6½ inches high as shown.

Join the zigzag blocks into border strips. Each side border has 11 zigzag units; the end border has eight units.

ASSEMBLY: To piece side panels and the center section, combine strips as shown in assembly diagram, *right.*

Sew the end border unit to the bottom of the center section, then add the remaining long red strips to each side.

Join the short white and green end strips; sew the two-strip combination to the bottom of the center section.

Sew remaining strips onto side zigzag borders as shown. Aligning top edges, join side panels to center.

FINISHING: Cut and piece backing fabric to match quilt top. *Note:* If backing fabric is not wide enough, it may be necessary to sew a 6-inch-wide piece of scrap fabric between the two panels of backing fabric.

Layer backing, batting, and quilt top. Quilt as desired. The quilt shown on page 49 has clamshells and circles

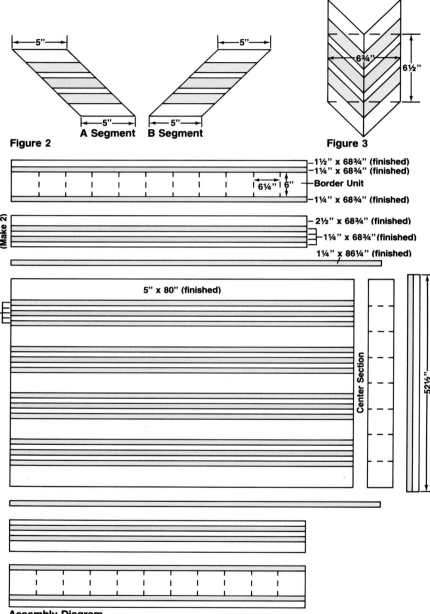

Figure 1

Figure 2   A Segment   B Segment

Figure 3

Assembly Diagram
STRIP QUILT

quilted in the wider white strips and a narrow undulating vine motif in the narrow strips. When quilting is complete, trim batting and backing even with the quilt top.

Make 1½-inch-wide binding (bias or straight) from remaining red fabric. Piece strips together to make approximately 10 yards of binding. Fold binding in half lengthwise, wrong sides together, to make a ¾-inch-wide strip.

Sew raw edges of binding to quilt edges, mitering corners. Turn binding over to back; hand-sew to backing.

Plaid Afghan

Shown on page 48.
Afghan measures approximately 50x67 inches.

MATERIALS

Tahki's Designer Homespun Tweed (100-gram skeins): 9 skeins of raspberry (207), 5 skeins of barley (222), and 1 skein of teal (213)
Size 10 circular needle (36 inches long)
Size H crochet hook
Tapestry needle
8 stitch markers

Abbreviations: See page 35.
Gauge: 14 stitches = 4 inches.

INSTRUCTIONS

Note: Work chart, *right,* in st st, reading chart from right to left on knit (right side) rows and left to right on purl (wrong side) rows. On right side, work A–B three times, then B–C once. Follow the same sequence on wrong-side rows.

With circular needle and raspberry yarn, cast on 195 stitches. Do not join.

Note: Work first 10 and last 10 stitches in garter stitch. Vertical teal strips are worked in duplicate stitch after afghan is completed.

Row 1: K 10 raspberry, place marker; ** k 25 with raspberry, place marker; attach small ball barley, * k 1 barley, k 1 raspberry; rep bet *s 12 times, k 1 barley; place marker.** Rep between **s 2 times more; k 25 raspberry; place marker, k 10 raspberry.

Rows 2–36: Continue to follow chart, working first and last 10 raspber-ry stitches in garter st pat, and working center 185 sts in st st.

Row 37: K 10 raspberry; ** attach small ball barley; * k 1 barley, k 1 raspberry; rep bet *s 12 times, k 1 bar-ley; k 25 with barley; rep between **s two times more; rep bet *s one time more; k 10 with raspberry.

Rows 38–53: Continue to follow chart, working from A–B three times and B–C once.

Row 54: K 10 raspberry, join teal and k 185, k 10 raspberry.

Row 55: K 10 raspberry, p 185 with teal, k 10 raspberry.

Rows 56–72: Continue to follow chart using both yarns, working from A–B three times and B–C once.

Repeat rows 1–72 as established three times more, then rep 1–36 once more. Bind off in raspberry.

FINISHING: Using crochet hook and raspberry yarn, sc in each st across top and bottom of afghan. Referring to chart, duplicate st (see stitch diagram on page 63) vertical lines of plaid with teal yarn. Weave in ends.

FRINGE: Cut four 15-inch lengths of raspberry yarn for every other sc st across top and bottom of afghan. Fold four lengths in half and use crochet hook to pull loop through sc. Pull fringe tails through fringe loop. Rep in every other st across both top and bot-tom of afghan.

Trim ends of fringe even.

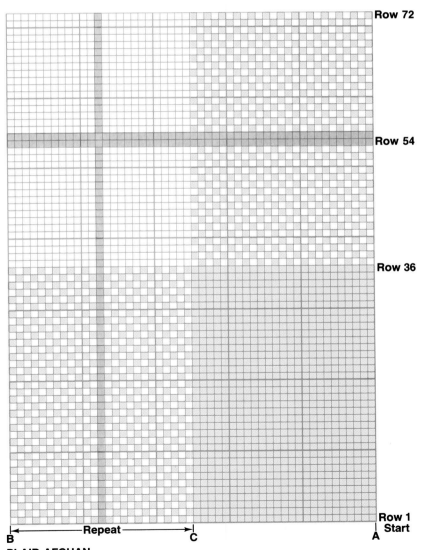

PLAID AFGHAN

Row 72

Row 54

Row 36

Row 1
Start
A

B — Repeat — C

Holiday Workshop

Here's our answer to the age-old question—is there really a Santa Claus?
"Yes, Virginia, there is a Santa Claus; he's knitted and stuffed, a real jolly old soul!"

Straight from the North Pole on quicksilver knitting needles (double-pointed ones that is), here's a "holly-jolly" figure of old St. Nick. He's guaranteed to be the attention getter in any crowd of toys and dolls.

The doll is knit in one piece, from his pink button nose to his high-topped black boots. Only the hat is stitched separately. Worked from the top down, the finished piece is stuffed firmly to stand 21½ inches tall among the packages and Christmas goodies.

Wool fleece makes an instant snowy beard and hair. Twinkly eyes and apple cheeks appear in a flash with simple duplicate stitches.

You'll sleep peacefully knowing that Santa will be back year after year to wish *"Merry Christmas to all, and to all a good night!"*

Complete instructions for the Santa doll begin on page 62.

61

Knitted Santa

Shown on page 60.
Finished Santa is 21½ inches tall.

MATERIALS

Harrisville 2-ply wool yarn (3.5-oz. skein): 2 skeins red (57), 1 skein *each* white (20), beige (40), and black (11); plus scraps of apple blossom (60) and cobalt (44)
Two sets of Size 2 double-point needles (dpn)
Size F crochet hook
Sheep's wool or fleece for hair
Polyester fiberfill
Tapestry needle
Small watch buckle
⅜ yard of green felt for bag
2 yards of gold cord

Abbreviations: See page 35.
Gauge: 7 sts = 1 inch.

INSTRUCTIONS

Note: This doll is knit on dpns. All rows are knitted unless otherwise specified. When instructions give increasing (inc) directions, *always* work the increase in the *next* stitch by knitting in the front, then the back of that stitch.

The knitting gauge is intentionally *tight* so the stuffing does not show through and the doll does not stretch out of shape.

HEAD: With beige yarn, cast on 30 sts. Divide sts onto three needles, taking care not to twist sts—10 sts each.

Rnd 1: K around.

Rnd 2: K 2, inc, (k 4, inc) 5 times, k 2—36 sts.

Rnds 3, 5, 7, 9, and 11: Knit.

Rnd 4: K 3, inc, k 4, inc, k 5, inc, k 6, inc, k 5, inc, k 4, inc, k 3—42 sts.

Rnd 6: K 4, inc, (k 5, inc) 2 times, k 8, inc, (k 5, inc) 2 times, k 4—48 sts.

Rnd 8: (K 5, inc) 2 times, k 6, inc, k 10, inc, k 6, (inc, k 5) 2 times—54 sts.

Rnd 10: (K 6, inc) 3 times, k 12, (inc, k 6) 3 times—60 sts.

Rnd 12: (K 7, inc) 2 times, k 6, inc, k 14, inc, k 6, (inc, k 7) 2 times—66 sts.

Rnds 13–29: Knit even.

Note: On the next 10 rnds, continue to work on the three needles. At the same time, work the instructions below for the sts on the second needle to shape the eyes and nose.

Rnd 30: K sts on first needle; on second needle k 7; using 20-inch dbl strand of cobalt yarn, **k in front and back of next st 2 times, sl first 3 sts just worked over the fourth st on needle—eye made;** with beige k 6, work eye in next st, with beige k 7; k sts on third needle.

Rnd 31: K even with beige, k each eye st as one—66 sts.

Rnd 32: K first needle sts; k 10, inc, k 11; k third needle sts—67 sts.

Rnd 33: K first needle sts; k 10, join apple blossom, inc, k 1, inc—beg nose; with beige k 10; k third needle sts.

Rnd 34: K first needle sts; k 10, with apple blossom, k 5, with beige, k 10; k third needle sts.

Rnd 35: K first needle sts; k 10, with apple blossom, inc, k 3, inc; with beige, k 10; k third needle sts.

Rnd 36: K first needle sts; k 10, with apple blossom, k 7; with beige, k 10; k third needle sts.

Rnd 37: K first needle sts; k 10, with apple blossom, inc, k 5, inc; with beige, k 10; k third needle sts.

Rnd 38: K sts on first needle; k 10, with apple blossom, k 9; with beige, k 10; k sts on third needle.

Rnd 39: K sts on first needle; k 11, with apple blossom, k 8 *loosely,* sl first 4 sts just worked over the last 4; with beige, k 10; k third needle sts.

Rnd 40: K around. When you get to the 4 strands of apple blossom, insert a crochet hook through the 4 strands of apple blossom and pull a beige strand and place loop on needle—66 sts.

Rnds 41–45: Knit even.

Rnd 46: (beg chin dec) (K 7, k 2 tog) 2 times, k 6, k 2 tog, k 14, k 2 tog, k 6, (k 2 tog, k 7) 2 times—60 sts.

Rnd 47: Knit even.

Rnd 48: (K 6, k 2 tog) 3 times, k 12, (k 2 tog, k 6) 3 times—54 sts.

Rnd 49: Knit even.

Rnd 50: (K 5, k 2 tog) 2 times; k 6, k 2 tog, k 10, k 2 tog, k 6, (k 2 tog, k 5) 2 times—48 sts.

Rnd 51: Knit even.

Rnd 52: K 4, k 2 tog, (k 5, k 2 tog) 2 times; k 8, k 2 tog, (k 5, k 2 tog) 2 times; k 4—42 sts.

Rnd 53: Knit even.

Rnd 54: K 3, k 2 tog, k 4, k 2 tog, k 5, k 2 tog, k 6, k 2 tog, k 5, k 2 tog, k 4, k 2 tog, k 3—36 sts.

Rnd 55: Knit even.

Rnd 56: K 2, k 2 tog, (k 4, k 2 tog) 5 times; k 2—30 sts.

Rnd 57: Knit even.

Rnd 58: K to last 5 sts, leave unworked, fasten off beige yarn; join dbl strand of white, k 5 sts.

Rnd 59: Inc 6 sts evenly spaced around; rearrange sts on needles so face center is between second and third needle, and back of head is first needle—12 sts on each needle.

SUIT: Purl 4 rnds even; fasten off dbl strand white.

Rnd 5: Join red, k *each white strand* across first (back) needle (24 sts); second needle, k 20 *white strands,* join dbl strand white, p last 2 white sts; third needle, p 2 white sts, join red, k 20 *white strands*—68 sts.

Rnd 6: Inc in every red st around; cont to p the 4 white sts—132 sts.

Rnd 7: K even.

Rnd 8: K around and rearrange sts onto 4 needles as follows: 38 sts on first—back, 26 sts on second—right shoulder, 42 sts on third—front, and 26 on fourth—left shoulder.

Rnds 9–28: Knit even. End last rnd at end of first needle.

RIGHT ARM: Knit 26 shoulder sts and rearrange on 3 needles as follows: k 10 sts; k 10 sts; k 6 sts and cast on 4 sts for underarm—30 sts.

Knit even for 30 rnds—approximately 6 inches.

Rnd 32: (K 3, k 2 tog) 6 times—24 sts; fasten off red.

Rnd 33: (cuff) Join dbl strand white, k around.

Rnds 34–37: Purl around. Fasten off white at end of Rnd 37.

Rnd 38: (mitten) Join black, k around—24 sts.

Rnd 39: (K 2, k 2 tog) 6 times—18 sts.

Rnds 40–47: Knit even.

Rnd 48: (K 2 tog, k 1) 6 times—12 sts.

Rnds 49 and 50: K 2 tog around—3 sts rem at end of Rnd 50; cut yarn. Use tapestry needle to thread yarn through 3 rem sts; pull tight and weave in tail.

LEFT ARM: On separate needle, cast on 4 sts with red. Knitting from sts for left shoulder, use this same needle to k across 6 sts; k across 10 sts with second needle; k across last 10 sts with third needle. Knit even for 30 rnds—approximately 6 inches.

Follow the instructions for the right arm to complete left arm.

BODY: With first needle and red yarn pick up and k 4 sts of right underarm and k across next 19 sts; with second needle, p 4 with dbl strand white, k 18 red; third needle, k 1, pick up and knit 4 sts of left underarm, k 16; fourth needle, k 22—88 sts.

K even for 1¾ inches. *Next rnd:* On first needle (k 2 tog, k 3) 4 times, k 2 tog, k 1—18 sts; second needle, p 4 white, k 2 tog across with red—13 sts; third needle, (k 3, k 2 tog) 4 times, k 1—17 sts; fourth needle, k 2, (k 2 tog, k 3) 4 times—18 sts—66 sts total.

Next rnd: With black, (k 31, k 2 tog) 2 times—64 sts.

BELT: K next 3 rnds even.

Rnd 4: (K 14, k 2 tog) 4 times—60 sts. End black yarn. Sew buckle to center of belt.

JACKET BOTTOM: Join red, * k 1, inc, * rep between *s to second needle; k 3 (double strand) white, with red inc in next 2 sts, k 1, inc in every other st; third and fourth needle, * k 1, inc, * rep across both needles—88 sts.

Next rnd: With red k 25, p 4 with white, k 59 with red. Cont until jacket bottom measures 2½ inches. End red before center white sts; p four rnds dbl strand white; bind off.

PANTS: Turn jacket bottom up to belt; with red pick up and k 60 sts beg in the center of the back and along bottom of the black belt sts—15 sts on each of the four needles. K even for 2¼ inches.

RIGHT LEG: K to center front, cast on 4 sts for crotch of pants, join to back needle on same (right) half of body—34 sts divided onto 3 needles. K evenly for 5 inches from crotch. Fasten off red leaving sts on needles.

Rep for left leg on opposite side.

BOOTS: Join black; k one rnd; p one rnd.

Next rnd: P around, inc 4 sts evenly spaced—38 sts.

Continue to p rnds for 2¼ inches. Dec 4 sts evenly on next rnd. Purl ¼ inch more. Knit 6 rnds; bind off.

Turn all of black tube up the leg. Starting in the center of the back of boot, pick up and k the 34 red p sts inside leg (next to black).

Next rnd: Dec 4 sts evenly spaced—30 sts, 10 sts on each needle.

Knit 6 rnds even.

Inc on the front (toe) needle in the next 6 rnds as follows:

Rnd 1: Inc in fourth and sixth sts.
Rnd 2: Inc in fifth and seventh sts.
Rnd 3: Inc in sixth and eighth sts.
Rnd 4: Inc in seventh and ninth sts.
Rnd 5: Inc in eighth and tenth sts.
Rnd 6: Inc in ninth and eleventh sts—42 sts.

Knit 8 rnds even. Arrange 21 sts from both sides of heel to toe on two needles; use Kitchener stitch to close seam. Rep for other boot.

STUFFING: Use a ruler to push stuffing through the head and down to boot toes. Stuff every part of Santa firmly; sew top of head opening closed.

HAT: Cast on 78 sts with white yarn onto 3 needles; join—26 sts on each needle. Knit 6 rnds even. Dec 6 sts evenly spaced around—72 sts. Knit 1 rnd more; end white. Join red yarn; inc 1 st in the center of all three needles—75 sts. Knit even for 2 inches. Next rnd, dec 3 sts evenly spaced—72 sts. Knit 2 rnds. Cont to dec 3 sts evenly spaced every third rnd until 42 sts rem. Then dec 3 sts every sixth rnd until 2 sts rem on each needle. Cut a 10-inch tail and thread through rem sts; pull sts tight and weave in tail. Make a 1-inch pom-pom with white yarn and attach to the point on the hat.

The white edge on the hat will roll over. Sew the rolled edge down to the beginning of the red part of the hat.

HAIR: Soak wool fleece in mild wool soap. Rinse fleece; air-dry. Sew fleece to face for beard and mustache.

Sew more fleece to head for hair. Place hat on Santa; tack hat to head around the white hat band.

FACIAL DETAILS: Embroider a red mouth between beard and mustache.

Referring to the chart *bottom,* duplicate st cheeks with apple blossom. See the stitch diagram, *below,* for duplicate stitch instructions.

Embroider eyebrows using white yarn in satin stitches. Add a French knot to one side of each eye to add a "twinkle." (Refer to page 156 for stitch diagrams.)

BAG: Using pinking shears, cut three 11x11-inch pieces from the green felt. Join the pieces into a three-sided tube. Treating the seamed side of the bag as the right side, gather the bottom of the bag; stitch the gathered bottom closed.

Using regular scissors, clip small holes for the ties approximately 1 inch from the top of the bag.

Cut gold cord in half. Weave one cord end through the openings until you return to the beginning. Knot the ends. Beginning at the opposite side of the bag, weave the second cord through the openings; knot ends.

Partially fill the bag with polyester fiberfill. Add small toys and packages at the top of the bag.

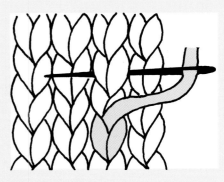

DUPLICATE STITCH

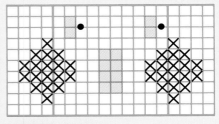

SANTA'S CHEEKS

A Wonderful White Christmas

Elegant white ornaments, toys, and accessories glisten all through the house like new-fallen snow on a cold winter night. Poinsettia reds and candy pinks add small splashes of color. Celebrate the joy of the season in splendid, sparkling white.

Crochet, paper, and other materials add to the romance of a frosty white-trimmed tree.

Tiers of baby's-breath circle the tree, providing a framework for a legion of white ornaments: large and small crocheted hearts; wax candy-mold hearts; and three scherenschnitte ornaments, including the flying angel at *right.*

Full-size patterns and illustrated instructions for all these ornaments begin on page 70.

64

Prancing white reindeer are magical messengers of Santa's imminent arrival, creating happy anticipation in eager young hearts.

Sleek stags dance face to face amid lacy cross-stitched snowflakes to proclaim the joys of the season, *right*. Sparkling white and bright red floss create a 15¼x17-inch design stitched over two threads of 26-count gray linen.

The high-stepping reindeer is easy for children to trace and cut from paper, *below*. Simply make a card-board template from the full-size pattern on page 74 and let them go to work. A team of the 6¾x8-inch ornaments flies through the twinkling lights of the icy white tree, *opposite*.

The tree is a wintry wonderland with ornaments of snow and ice. A "snowball" garland of foam balls encircles the glowing structure. The starbursts are made with wooden skewers radiating from a center of painted modeling clay. A dusting of glitter completes the icicle effect.

The cheeriness of Christmas red is introduced in the patchwork Maple Leaf quilt, *opposite*. The square and triangle shapes are easy to sew by hand or machine. Four leaf stems come together in the center of each block to create a striking design. The finished quilt is 73½ inches square.

The dashing reindeer reappear in a wood-crafted coffee table, topped with an 18x38-inch piece of glass. Plywood and dowels are the basic supplies needed to create this unique piece of furniture.

See pages 74–78 for the directions and patterns for the projects on these pages.

A soft gray background emphasizes the white reindeer and snowflakes on this knitted holiday sweater, *right.* By knitting with two needle sizes, you create the dual texture of the design.

Chart and instructions for the sweater are on pages 72 and 73.

A scrap of lace-trimmed white fabric brings the Snowbaby Dolls to life, *below.* These lighthearted dolls can be puppets, cuddly friends, or sweet tree

toppers (see photograph on page 67). A small piece of fiberfill forms the head, and knotted corners make the arms. This is a terrific no-sew project that's great for bazaars and crafts fairs.

Snowbaby Doll directions are on page 75.

Elegant white moiré fabric sets off this jewel-and-lace pillow, *opposite.* A beautiful gift for the romantically inclined, it's graced with a petaled heart motif of lace trimmed with tiny seed pearls. Additional pearls are sewn randomly on the pillow's ruffled edging.

Helpful stitching diagrams and a full-size pattern for the Battenberg-style lace are included with the pillow instructions on page 79.

FULL-SIZE PATTERNS

SCHERENSCHNITTE ORNAMENTS

Scherenschnitte Ornaments

Shown on pages 64 and 65.
Finished ornaments are 3–4 inches long.

MATERIALS

White bond or parchment paper
Hard-lead pencil
Utility knife
Sharp scissors

INSTRUCTIONS

Trace the full-size patterns at *left* onto paper. Place each tracing on a cardboard cutting surface. Use a needle or pin to prick the dots on the angel design. Using a utility knife, cut small slits around the angel's face and wings and the dove's eye. Using small sharp scissors, cut away the shaded areas inside the designs, working from the center toward the outside. Cut away the perimeters of the designs last.

Wax Heart Ornaments

Shown on page 65.

MATERIALS

½ pound of white tallow wax (available through crafts supply stores or Gerlacho of Lecha, P.O. Box 213, Emmaus, PA 18049)
White crayon
3½ yards of ¼-inch-wide ribbon
12 flat-backed chocolate molds
2-pound coffee can
Large pan to hold coffee can
Plastic wrap
Wooden spoon, paring knife
Measuring cup or small pitcher

INSTRUCTIONS

Caution: Wax is flammable; heat just enough to melt wax. In case of fire, douse with baking soda. Use old utensils; wax is difficult to remove.

Protect work surface with newspaper covered with plastic wrap. Melt wax in a coffee can set in a pan filled with simmering water. Add white crayon to make the wax more opaque. Stir the melted wax with a wooden spoon.

For the ornament hangers, cut the ribbon into 10-inch lengths. Fold each length in half to form loops. Dip 1 inch of the cut ends into the wax to keep the ribbon ends together; set aside to dry.

Pour 1 cup of melted wax into a measuring cup. Pour wax into the molds, filling them to the rim. Insert ribbon hangers, holding them several seconds until wax begins to harden.

Allow ornaments to harden completely before removing them from the molds (about 15 minutes). Pop them out of the molds; trim any rough edges with a paring knife.

Fabric Heart Ornaments

Shown on page 65.
Finished ornaments are approximately 5½ inches across at the widest point.

MATERIALS
For each heart
Piece of embroidered fabric such as an old pillowcase or dresser scarf
⅔ yard of picot lace
Polyester fiberfill

INSTRUCTIONS
To make a heart pattern, fold a piece of paper in half. Sketch half a heart that measures approximately 3 inches at the widest point on the folded paper. You can use a coffee cup to trace the outline of a circle, then sketch the rest of the shape. Cut out the heart.

Using your pattern, cut a heart from the embroidered portion of the fabric. Cut a matching heart back from the plain area of the fabric.

Baste lace on the ¼-inch seam line around the embroidered heart. With right sides facing, stitch front to back, leaving an opening for turning. Clip seam allowances; turn right side out. Stuff, then stitch the opening closed.

Use ribbon or thread to make a hanging loop at the top of the heart.

Crocheted Openwork Heart Ornament

Shown on page 65.
Finished ornament is approximately 4½ inches across at the widest point.

MATERIALS
DMC Cébélia crochet cotton, Size 10
Size 6 steel crochet hook

Abbreviations: See page 35.
Gauge: 9 dc = 1 inch.

INSTRUCTIONS
Ch 8, join with sl st to form ring.

Rnd 1: Ch 5, dc in ring, (ch 3, trc in ring) 7 times; ch 3, dc in ring, ch 2, sl st in third st of beg ch-5.

Rnd 2: Ch 3, dc in next dc, ch 3, in first trc work (trc, ch 3) 4 times; trc in same st; trc in next trc, ch 2, trc in next trc, ch 3, in next trc work (trc, ch 3) 3 times; trc in same st; ch 3, trc in next trc, ch 2, trc in next trc, in next trc work (trc, ch 3) 4 times; trc in same st; ch 3, dc in last dc, ch 3, sl st in sl st at end of Rnd 1.

Rnd 3: Work 3 sc in ch-3, sc in dc, 3 hdc over next ch-3, (dc in next trc, 5 dc over ch-3) 3 times; dc in next trc, 3 dc over ch-3, dc in trc, hdc in next trc, 2 sc over ch-2, (sc in trc, 3 sc over ch-3) twice; hdc in trc, 5 dc over ch-3 at tip of heart. Continue up other side: Hdc in trc, (3 sc over ch-3, sc in trc) twice; 2 sc over ch-2, hdc in trc, dc in next trc, 3 dc over ch-3, (dc in trc, 5 dc over ch-3) 3 times, dc in trc, 3 hdc over ch-3, sc in dc, 3 sc over last ch-3, sl st in first sc made.

Rnd 4: Sl st in second, third, and fourth sc, ch 7, sk 3 hdc, trc in first dc, (ch 5, sk 2 dc, trc in next dc) 6 times; (ch 5, sk 3 sts, trc in next st) 4 times, ch 5, make (trc, ch 5, trc) in center dc of point, ch 5, sk 2 dc, trc in hdc, (ch 5, sk 3 sts, trc in next st) 4 times; (ch 5, sk 2 dc, trc in next dc) 6 times; ch 3, sk 3 hdc, trc in sc, sl st in fourth st of ch-7.

Rnd 5: Make 3 sc over ch-3 sp, then work in each ch-5 sp as follows: Make (3 dc, ch 3, sl st in top of last dc just made for picot, 3 dc in same sp) all around, then make 3 sc in last ch-3 sp. Sl st in the first sc made. Fasten off.

Filet-Crocheted Heart Ornaments

Shown on page 65.
Finished ornaments are approximately 4½ inches across at the widest point.

MATERIALS
DMC Cébélia crochet cotton, Size 10
Size 6 steel crochet hook

Abbreviations: See page 35.
Gauge: 9 dc = 1 inch.

INSTRUCTIONS
FIRST SECTION: *Row 1:* Ch 4, 4 dc in fourth ch from hook; ch 3, turn.

Row 2: 2 dc in first dc, ch 1, sk dc, dc in next dc, ch 1, sk dc, 3 dc in top of turning-ch; ch 3, turn.

Row 3: 2 dc in first dc, ch 1, sk dc, dc in next dc, (dc in ch-1 sp, dc in next dc) twice; ch 1, sk dc, 3 dc in top of turning-ch; ch 3, turn.

Rows 4–7: 2 dc in first dc, ch 1, sk dc, dc in next dc, dc in ch-1 sp, dc in each dc across center section, dc in ch-1 sp, dc in next dc, ch 1, sk dc, 3 dc in top of turning-ch; ch 3, turn. There will be 21 dc in center section of Row 7.

Row 8: Sk first dc, dc in next 2 dc, ch 1, dc in each 21 dc, ch 1, dc in last 2 dc and in top of turning-ch; ch 3, turn.

Row 9: Sk first dc, dc in next 2 dc, ch 1, dc in next 9 dc, (ch 1, sk dc, dc in next dc) twice; dc in rem 8 dc of center, ch 1, dc in last 2 dc and in top of turning-ch; turn.

continued

FILET-CROCHETED HEART

Row 10: Sl st in second dc, ch 3, dc in next dc and in ch-1 sp, ch 1, sk dc, dc in each of next 6 dc, ch 1; sk next dc, **holding back on hook last lp of each st, make dc in next dc and in ch-1 sp, yo and pull through all lps on hook—2-dc cluster made;** turn.

Row 11: Ch 3, dc in ch-1 sp, (dc in next dc, ch 1, sk next dc) 3 times, dc in ch-1 sp and in next 2 dc, turn.

Row 12: Sl st in second dc, ch 3, (dc in next dc and in ch-1 sp) 3 times, dc in next 2 dc, ch 3, sl st in top of turning-ch of previous row; make sl st in side of same turning-ch and in top of cluster of Row 10; ch 3, sl st in center dc of Row 9; do not fasten off.

SECOND TOP SECTION: *Row 10:* Ch 3, make 2-dc cluster in ch-1 sp and first dc, ch 1, sk dc, dc in each of next 6 dc, ch 1, sk next dc, dc in ch-1 sp and next 2 dc; turn.

Row 11: Sl st in second dc, ch 3, dc in next dc and in ch-1 sp, (ch 1, sk dc, dc in next dc) 3 times; dc in ch-1 sp and in cluster st; ch 3, turn.

Row 12: Sk first dc, dc in next 2 dc, (dc in ch-1 sp, dc in next dc) 3 times; dc in next dc. This row will have 9 dc plus the turning-ch; do not fasten off.

EDGING: *Rnd 1:* (Ch 5, sc in top corner of previous row) 11 times; ch 5, dc in point of heart, (ch 5, sc in top corner of next row) 12 times; (ch 5, sk 2 dc, sc in next dc) 3 times; ch 5, sc in top corner of Row 11, ch 2, dc in top of Row 10, on other section, ch 2, sc in top of Row 11, ch 5, sc in top corner of Row 12, (ch 5, sk 2 dc, sc in next dc) 3 times.

Rnd 2: Sl st to center of next ch-5 lp, (ch 5, sc in next lp) 11 times; ch 5, make (dc, ch 5, dc) in dc at point; (ch 5, sc in next lp) 16 times, ch 2, dc bet the 2 dc at center, ch 2, (sc in next ch-5 lp, ch 5) 4 times; sl st to beg of rnd.

Rnd 3: Make (sc, hdc, dc, ch 3, sl st in top of dc just made for picot, hdc, sc) in each ch-5 lp around. At top of heart make 2 sc in each of the ch-2 sps. After last scallop is completed, join with sl st in first sc on rnd and fasten off.

Small Crocheted Heart Ornament

Shown on page 65.
Finished heart is approximately 2½ inches across at the widest point.

MATERIALS
DMC Cébélia crochet cotton, Size 10
Size 6 steel crochet hook

Abbreviations: See page 35.
Gauge: 9 dc = 1 inch.

INSTRUCTIONS
BODY: *Row 1:* Ch 17, dc in eighth ch from hook, (ch 2, sk 2 ch, dc in next ch) 3 times; ch 5, turn.

Row 2: (Dc in next dc, ch 2) 3 times; sk 2 ch of turning-ch, dc in next ch; ch 5, turn.

Rows 3 and 4: Rep Row 2; do not ch 5 at end of Row 4.

Working down side of block, make 2 sc around post of last dc made, *sc in end of next row, ch 7, sk end of next row, sc in end of next row*, 5 sc over corner ch-5 sp, rep bet *s once more; 2 sc around post of next dc, sl st in corner st of same block; turn.

Row 5: In next ch-7 lp work (trc, ch 1) 11 times, sl st in center sc of 5 sc-grp; ch 1, in next ch-7 lp work (trc, ch 1) 11 times; sk next 2 sts, sl st in next st. Do not turn.

EDGING: Continuing around edge of heart and working around posts, make 2 sc around next post, **ch 3, sl st in sc just made—picot made,** sc around same post, sc in end of next row; *around next post work sc, picot, sc; sc in end of next row*; rep bet *s once more. In ch-5 corner lp work sc, picot, 2 sc, picot, 2 sc, picot, and sc; sc in end of next row; rep bet *s 3 times—9 picots made; work sc in ch-1 sp; (sc in next trc, picot, sc in next ch-1 sp) 11 times; ch 25 for hanger; sc in next ch-1 sp; rep bet ( )s 11 times; join to sc at beg of edging rnd and fasten off.

Reindeer Sweater
Shown on page 68.
Directions for Size 40; changes for sizes 44, 48, and 52 follow in parentheses.

MATERIALS
Brunswick Pearl: 9 skeins MC—gray (5915) and 4 skeins Color A—white (5900)
3 skeins Color B—Windmist white (2800)
Sizes 3 and 5 knitting needles (Sizes 4 and 6, sizes 5 and 7, and sizes 6 and 8)
3 bobbins
Yarn needle

Abbreviations: See page 35.
Gauge: With larger needle over st st, 21 sts = 4 inches (20 sts = 4 inches, 18 sts = 4 inches, 17 sts = 4 inches). Be sure to check gauge; use any size needles that will produce gauge given.

INSTRUCTIONS
Note: Sweater is designed to be over-size. Width across back or front: 22 inches (23, 25½, 27 inches); width of sleeve at upper arm: 18 inches (19, 20, 21½ inches); length of sleeve seam: 18 inches, all sizes. All sizes are worked with the same number of stitches.

Note: Snowflakes and reindeer's eye are added with duplicate stitch after the front and back are completed.

■ **Working the Front**
Start at lower edge with larger needles and yarn B; cast on 110 sts. Change to small needles; work in k 1, p 1 ribbing for 3 inches, increasing 4 sts evenly spaced on last row—114 sts; fasten off B. Join A. With large needles, work in st st (knit 1 row, p 1 row) for 20 rows.

Wind two bobbins with A and one bobbin with MC. When changing colors, always twist the color not in use around the other to prevent holes; drop color not in use to wrong side of work. Follow each right-side row on chart, *below right,* from right to left, each wrong-side row from left to right.

Starting with Row 1, follow chart to within last 13 sts, drop A; with MC bobbin k 4; with bobbin A, k 9. Hereafter, use bobbins as necessary. Follow chart until Row 121 is completed.

FIRST NECK SHAPING: *Next row:* Work Row 122 until 45 sts on right-hand needle; slip remaining sts on a stitch holder. Turn.

Next 5 rows: Following chart, dec one st at neck edge every row—40 sts. Remaining sts are not shown on chart.

Next 4 rows: Work even.

FIRST SHOULDER SHAPING:

Row 1: Bind off first 10 sts; complete row.

Row 2: Work even.

Rows 3–6: Rep last 2 rows twice; bind off.

SECOND NECK SHAPING: With wrong side facing, sl next 24 sts onto a shorter holder, sl rem 45 sts onto larger needle; join MC at neck edge.

Next row: Work across.

Following 5 rows: Follow chart.

Next 3 rows: Work even over 40 sts.

SECOND SHOULDER SHAPING: Rep first shoulder shaping.

■ **Working the Back**
Work as for front until ribbing is completed—114 sts. Change to larger needles and yarn A. Work same as for Front next 30 rows.

Row 31: K 1 A, k 113 MC. Drop A. With MC only work in st st until length is same as front to shoulder shaping.

SHOULDER SHAPING: When the length is the same as front to shoulder shaping, bind off 10 sts at beg of each of next 8 rows. Slip rem 34 sts to holder for Back Neck.

■ **Working the Sleeves**
With larger needles and color B, cast on 40 sts. Change to smaller needles; work in k 1, p 1 ribbing for 3 inches, inc 16 sts evenly spaced across last row—56 sts; fasten off B. Join A. Wind 2 bobbins with A, 1 bobbin with MC. Change to larger needles.

Row 1 (right side): K.

Row 2: P.

Rows 3–4: Work even.

Row 5: Inc 1 st at each end—58 sts.

Rows 6–13: Work even in st st, inc 1 st at each end of rows 9 and 13—62 sts at end of Row 13.

Row 14: P 9 A, p 4 MC, p 49 A.

Row 15: K 46 A, k 8 MC, k 8 A.

Row 16: P 8 A, p 8 MC, p 46 A.

Row 17: Inc 1 st in first st, k next 42 sts A, k 12 MC, k 6 A, inc 1 st in last st—64 sts.

Row 18: P 7 A, p 15 MC, p 28 A, p 8 MC, p 6 A.

Row 19: K 5 A, k 17 MC, k 18 A, k 18 MC, k 6 A.

Row 20: P 6 A, p 20 MC, p 11 A, p 23 MC, p 4 A.

Row 21: Inc 1 st in first st, k next 2 sts A, k 24 MC, k 8 A, k 24 MC, k 4 A, inc 1 st in last st—66 sts.

Row 22: P 5 A, p 25 MC, p 4 A, p 28 MC, p 4 A.

Row 23: K 3 A, k 59 MC, k 4 A.

Row 24: P 3 A, p 61 MC, p 2 A. Fasten off A.

Row 25: Inc 1 st at each end—68 sts.

With MC only, work in st st. Inc 1 st at each end every fourth row until 94 sts are on the needle. Work even until sleeve is 18 inches long. Bind off.

■ **Duplicate Stitch**
One snowflake is positioned on the chart; add more snowflakes in duplicate stitch randomly with yarn A. Duplicate stitch five to seven snowflakes randomly on both Front and Back. Work three snowflakes on each sleeve.

Work the reindeer's eye in duplicate st with MC.

■ **Assembly and Finishing**
Sew the left shoulder seam. With smaller needle and MC k sts on back holder, pick up and k 1 st in end st of each row along neck edge, k sts on front holder, pick up and k 1 st in end st of each row along neck edge, having a total number of sts divisible by 2. Work in k 1, p 1 ribbing for 2½ inches. With larger needle, bind off.

Sew right shoulder seam. With center top of sleeve at shoulder seam, sew in sleeves. Sew side and sleeve seams.

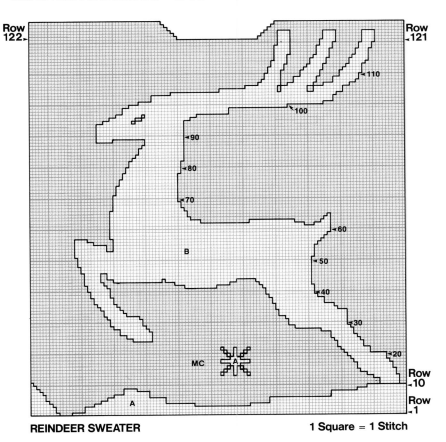

REINDEER SWEATER   **1 Square = 1 Stitch**

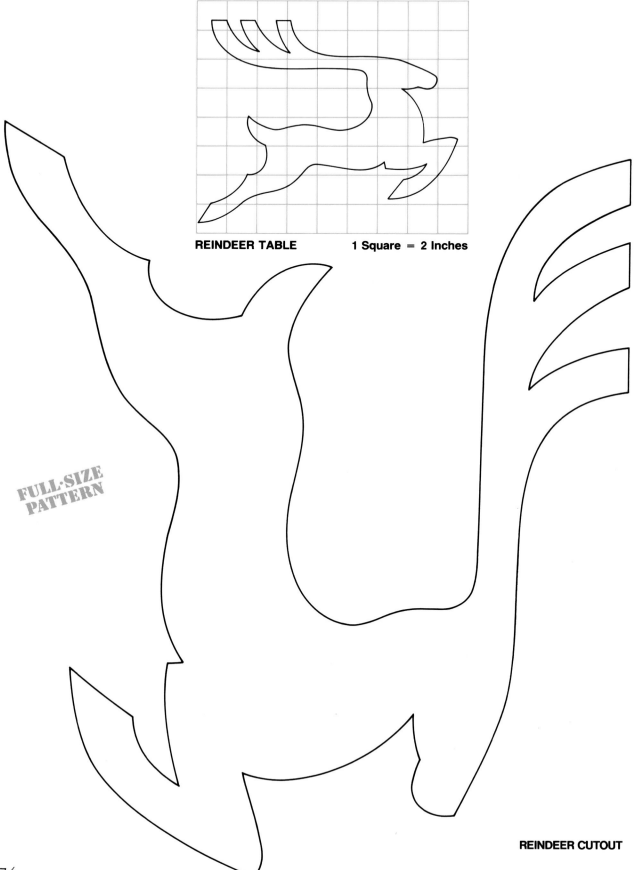

REINDEER TABLE   1 Square = 2 Inches

FULL·SIZE PATTERN

REINDEER CUTOUT

Reindeer Cutouts

Shown on pages 66 and 67.
Finished ornaments are 6¾x8 inches.

MATERIALS
Heavy white paper
Small sharp scissors
Needle and monofilament (optional)

INSTRUCTIONS
Trace the full-size deer pattern, *opposite*, onto heavy white paper. Using small sharp scissors, cut out the design.

Set the ornament in the tree or pierce the top of the design with a needle and hang with monofilament.

Reindeer Table

Shown on page 67.
Finished tabletop is 18x38 inches.

MATERIALS
4x8-foot piece of ¾-inch birch
  plywood
Two 15-inch-long ½-inch-diameter
  dowels
Wood glue
18x38-inch glass tabletop with
  rounded corners
16x40-inch piece of paper
Wood filler
White paint

INSTRUCTIONS
Enlarge the reindeer design, *opposite top*, onto paper. To complete the design, trace a reverse of the drawing and match with the first reindeer so the knees overlap. Refer to the photograph on page 67 for detail.

Crosscut plywood into four 17-inch segments. Trace pattern onto wood; cut four sets of reindeer. Stack reindeer so pieces align; drill a ½-inch hole through the centers of the front shoulders and rumps of all pieces.

Slide the dowels through the holes, spacing the deer evenly (about 4 inches apart); glue the dowels in place.

Fill the edges of the cutouts; sand and paint as desired. When dry, lay the glass tabletop on the reindeer.

Snowbaby Doll

Shown on page 68.

MATERIALS
24x24-inch square of white eyelet or
  lace fabric
¾ yard of assorted ribbons and laces
2 yards of ⅛-inch-wide satin ribbon
Purchased lace neckline insert for
  bonnet
Scraps of embroidery floss and white
  pearl cotton
Polyester fiberfill
Powdered blush

INSTRUCTIONS
Finish the raw edges of the fabric with a narrow hem. Sew ribbons and laces to the edges as desired.

Measure 5 inches down from the center of one edge; embroider the face here using French knots and long stitches. (See photograph on page 68 for suggestions on facial details.) Place a small ball of fiberfill behind the face; wrap the face around the fiberfill to form the head. Tie the neck with pearl cotton; trim ends.

Wrap the lace insert around the head to form a bonnet. Sew six strands of embroidery floss just under the brim of the bonnet, blending the floss colors and looping the floss as desired.

Knot the upper corners to form the doll's arms.

Starburst Ornament

Shown on page 67.

MATERIALS
Modeling clay
12 long wooden barbecue skewers
White latex semigloss spray paint
White or clear glitter

INSTRUCTIONS
Mold the modeling clay into a 1½-inch ball. Cut the skewers in half; insert skewers into clay ball in a spokelike fashion. Let dry completely.

Spray ornament with paint. While the paint is still wet, shake glitter over the ornament; let dry.

Snowball Garland

Shown on page 67.

MATERIALS
Plastic-foam balls in various sizes
String
Long doll needle with a large eye

INSTRUCTIONS
Roll the foam balls on a hard surface to give them a slightly uneven shape. Cut the string to desired length. Using a doll needle, thread the string through the center of the balls. Knot the ends around the last ball to secure them.

Reindeer Sampler

Shown on page 66.
Finished size is 15¼x17 inches.
Stitch count is 197 high by 220 wide.

MATERIALS
24-inch square of 26-count gray linen
DMC embroidery floss: 11 skeins of
  white, 2 skeins of red (321)
Embroidery hoop
Scissors
Graph paper and pencils

INSTRUCTIONS
The pattern and color key for the sampler are on pages 76 and 77. Chart the left half of the sampler onto graph paper; chart a mirror image for the right half of the sampler. Position the second half of the greeting as indicated on the graph.

Bind the edges of the linen with masking tape or turn under a hem.

Measure 4½ inches down from the top and 3 inches in from the left side of the linen; begin stitching the upper left corner of the border here. Use three plies of floss and work the cross-stitches over two threads of fabric.

When stitching is complete, steampress the stitchery on the wrong side. Frame the sampler as desired.

REINDEER SAMPLER

COLOR KEY   ▨ **White**   ☐ **Red (321)**

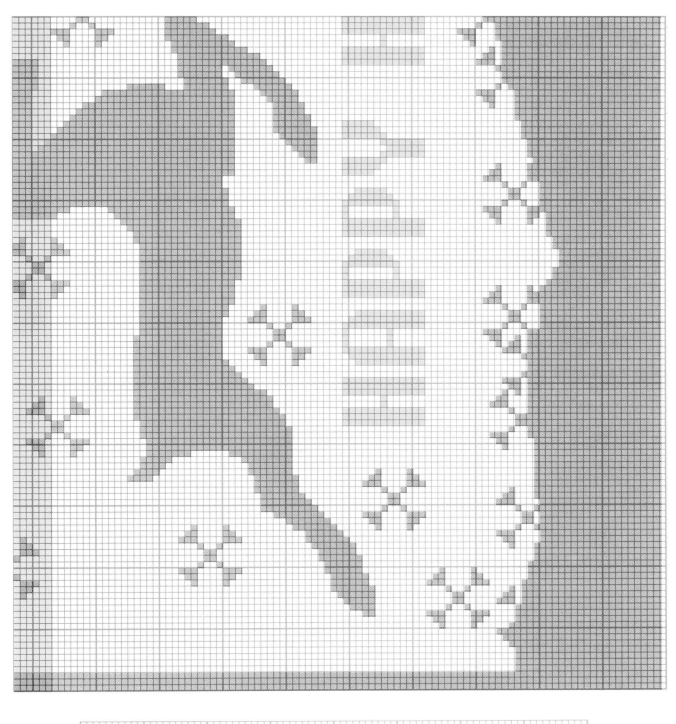

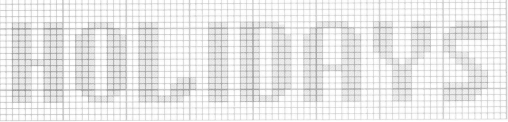

Maple Leaf Quilt

Shown on page 67.
Finished quilt is 73½ inches square. Each finished quilt block is 15 inches square.

MATERIALS

4¼ yards of red solid fabric for patchwork, border, and binding
3¾ yards of white or muslin fabric
4½ yards of backing fabric
Quilt batting
Cardboard or plastic for templates
Graph paper and pencil

INSTRUCTIONS

Unless otherwise stated, take ¼-inch seams and sew pieces with right sides facing. Template patterns are finished size; add ¼-inch seam allowances when cutting pieces from fabric. Border and sashing strip measurements include seam allowances. Trim them to length when they are added to the quilt.

TEMPLATES: On graph paper, draw a 2½-inch square for template B, a right-angle triangle with 2½-inch legs for template A, and a right-angle triangle with 5-inch legs for template C.

CUTTING: From red fabric, cut four 2x71-inch borders. Cut 18 block trim strips, each 1¼x15½ inches, and 18 block trim pieces, each 1¼x17 inches. Cut 36 stem pieces, each 1⅜x5 inches. Adding ¼-inch seam allowances, cut 216 A triangles and 36 C triangles. Set remaining red fabric aside for binding.

From white fabric, cut four 3x76-inch strips for outer borders and four 3x69-inch strips for the inner borders. Cut two 6x62-inch sashing strips and six 6x17-inch sashing strips. Adding ¼-inch seam allowances to all sides, cut 144 A triangles and 72 B squares.

BLOCK PIECING: The leaf shown in Figure 1, *above right,* is one-fourth of the finished Maple Leaf block.

Press long sides of one stem piece in toward the center so the strip measures approximately ½ inch wide. Pin a stem diagonally from corner to corner on a B square as shown in Figure 1. Appliqué stem; trim stem excess even with the edges of the square.

Sew a red A triangle to two adjacent sides of the B square to form a large

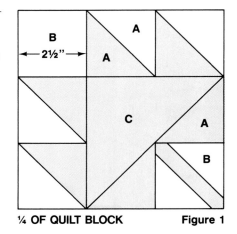

¼ OF QUILT BLOCK   Figure 1

triangle. Sew this pieced triangle to the red C triangle to form a square.

Join one red A triangle to a white one to form a triangle-square; make four triangle-squares. Assemble pieced segments to make one quarter-block.

To make a full block, join four quarter-blocks with the stems meeting at the center as illustrated in Figure 2, *below.* Make nine complete blocks.

ASSEMBLY: *Note:* Refer to Figure 2 for assembly. Sizes noted on the diagram are finished sizes of pieces.

To add red sashing, sew short strips to opposite sides of a block; sew longer strips to remaining sides. Repeat for all blocks. Blocks should now measure 17 inches, including seam allowances.

Join three blocks into a row, sewing the 6x17-inch white sashing strips between blocks. Make three rows.

Join all rows, sewing the long white sashing strips between rows; trim sashing fabric even with blocks.

Sew inner borders to quilt top and bottom; trim. Sew remaining inner borders to sides; trim. Repeat to add red borders and white outer borders.

FINISHING: Piece backing fabric to fit quilt top. Layer and baste top, batting, and back; quilt as desired.

Cut 9 yards of 2¼-inch-wide binding strips from remaining red fabric. Press binding in half, wrong sides facing, to measure 1⅛ inches wide. Bind edges with doubled binding.

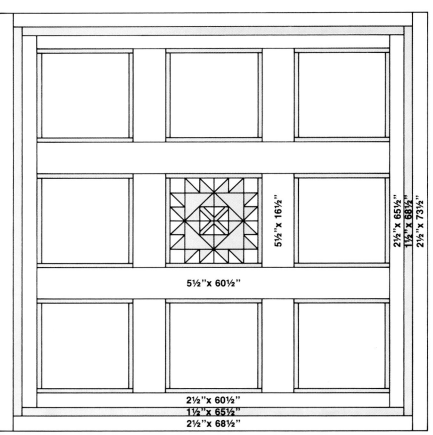

MAPLE LEAF QUILT   **Figure 2**

Battenberg Lace Heart Pillow

Shown on page 69.
Pillow, including ruffle, is approximately 14x16 inches. Lace motif is 5½x8 inches.

MATERIALS

1⅔ yards of 8-millimeter lace tape
1 yard of white taffeta moiré
½ yard of fleece
1 yard of narrow cording (piping)
Pearl beads
Polyester fiberfill
Nonpermanent marker
No. 12 pearl cotton thread
Brown paper bag, tissue paper

INSTRUCTIONS

Trace the full-size pattern, *below, far right,* onto brown paper; make a mirror image to complete the design.

Pull the gathering thread on one side of the tape; pin the tape to the paper pattern, making a small dart at the bottom of each heart and leaf. Baste the tape to the paper. Turn raw ends under; hem to prevent raveling.

Using pearl cotton and referring to Sorrento Wheel diagram, *below right,* start the center motif at the top of the inner heart (A). Go to the bottom of the heart (B) and take a stitch to secure the dart. Wind the thread back up to the center (see Winding Stitch diagram, *below right*). Take a stitch to the left side of the heart; wind the thread back to the center again. Repeat for all the spikes, ending with I to C.

Start the wheel by going under C and over F, under D and over H, etc. Repeat the full circle three times; then, wind the thread back to A and secure. Go to J, securing the edges of the tape on the way. Loosely stitch back and forth around the hearts, sewing from dot to dot (see full-size pattern, *far right*). Secure thread at K.

Referring to the Gathered Straight Stitch diagram, *above right,* gather bundles of five threads. With a new thread, secure the edge of the leaf tape and go to the middle of the first leaf. Take a stitch at the end of the leaf to secure the dart. Wind the thread back to the first vein; take a stitch to the end; wind the thread back. Repeat for all leaves.

Working from the wrong side, remove the basting threads. Rinse in cold water and lay flat until dry.

ASSEMBLY: Draw a heart shape onto tissue paper to accommodate the lace design, adding approximately 2 inches around the design. Transfer the design to the right side of the taffeta. Back the taffeta with fleece; stitch the layers together on the heart outline. Cut out, adding a ½-inch seam allowance. Cut a matching heart for the pillow back.

Center the lace heart on the pillow top; tack in place. Sew pearls to the lace heart in the positions indicated with open circles on the pattern.

For the ruffle, cut two 7x45-inch strips of taffeta. Sew the short ends together, forming a loop. Press the ruffle in half lengthwise, wrong sides facing. Gather the ruffle on the raw edge.

Cut a 1¾-inch-wide bias taffeta strip 36 inches long; cover cording with bias strip to make piping. Baste piping, then ruffle to the pillow top.

With right sides facing, stitch the pillow top to the back, leaving an opening for turning. Trim seams and clip curves; turn. Stuff the pillow, then sew the opening closed. Randomly sew pearls to the ruffle.

GATHERED STRAIGHT STITCH

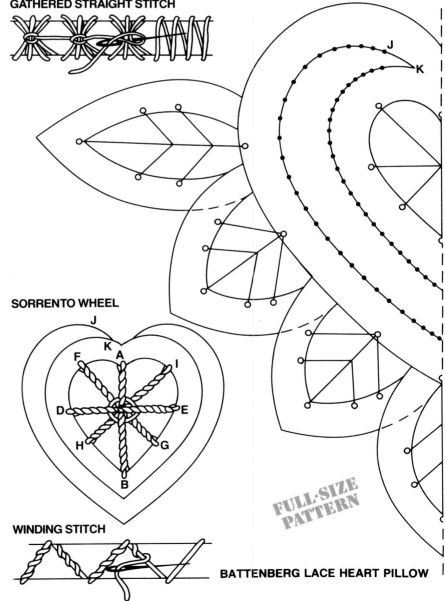

SORRENTO WHEEL

WINDING STITCH

FULL-SIZE PATTERN

BATTENBERG LACE HEART PILLOW

Holiday Workshop

Finding the perfect tree is a happy Christmas chore. Plant green, brown, and red scraps on a shaded patchwork prairie and you'll have a quilted forest of festive pines.

A small quilt of patchwork prairie pines is a holiday wall hanging and a year-round knee warmer or lap quilt.

Adapted from a pattern popular in the 1930s, this 9¾-inch block is pieced in straight diagonal lines into two half-blocks. Joined with a center seam and assembled with plain setting triangles, the finished quilt is 56¼x70 inches.

The wonderful interplay of scrap fabrics gives this quilt a lively sense of a real forest in which no two trees are exactly alike. A different fabric is used for each of the 18 trees, which are set against a background of assorted tan prints.

The variety of light, medium, and dark tans, randomly pieced into the blocks, is the essential ingredient for this quilt's magic.

A gay plaid border is the perfect frame for this forest, blending all the colors of the quilt with the rusty red and gold of autumn leaves.

Prairie Pines Quilt

Shown on pages 80 and 81.
Finished wall hanging is approximately
56¼x70 inches.
Finished block is 9¾ inches square.

MATERIALS

3 yards total of assorted tan print
    fabrics for background
⅛ yard or scraps of 18 assorted
    green, brown, and deep red print
    fabrics for trees
Scraps of assorted brown print fabrics
    for trunks
1¾ yards of red print fabric for inner
    borders and binding
1¾ yards of plaid fabric for border
¼ yard of dark gold print fabric for
    border corners
2¼ yards of 60-inch-wide muslin for
    quilt back
Quilt batting
Cardboard or plastic for templates
Graph paper
Tracing paper

INSTRUCTIONS

Trace and make cardboard or plastic
templates for the pattern pieces, *opposite*. The patterns for the patchwork
block are finished size; add ¼-inch
seam allowances to all pieces when cutting them from fabric.

CUT SETTING TRIANGLES: Make
patterns for the large setting triangles
and corner triangles. Cutting instructions for these patterns include seam
allowances and are slightly larger than
is needed. The triangles will be
trimmed before the borders are added
to the quilt.

For these large triangles, draw a 15-
inch square on graph paper. Divide the
square diagonally both ways into four
triangles. Make a template for one triangle to use to cut the setting triangles.

From the assorted tan print fabrics,
cut a total of 10 large triangles, placing
the template so the longest side of the
triangle is on the fabric grain.

For the corner triangles, draw a 10-
inch square on graph paper. Divide the
square diagonally into two triangles.
Make a template of one triangle for the
corner setting triangles.

From the assorted tan fabrics, cut
four corner triangles, placing the short
sides of the triangle template on the
fabric grain.

CUT BORDERS AND BINDING:
Measurements for the border pieces
include seam allowances. The borders
are cut longer than is needed; trim borders to the exact length when they are
added to the quilt top.

From the red print fabric, cut four
2½x60-inch borders. From plaid fabric, cut four 5½x60-inch borders.

From the gold fabric, cut four 7½-
inch squares for the border corners.

CUT BLOCK PIECES: The number
of pieces to cut for one block is listed
first, with the number of pieces to cut
for the entire wall hanging following
in parentheses.

From the assorted tan print fabrics,
cut two (36) *each* of triangles E and F.
Cut one (18) of piece H. Turn template H *wrong* side up and cut one (18)
reverse H piece. Cut three (54) G
pieces. Turn template G *wrong* side up
and cut three (54) reverse G pieces.

From the assorted tree fabrics, cut
four (72) A pieces and two (36) *each* of
piece B and piece C.

From the trunk fabrics, cut one (18)
D piece and one (18) reverse D piece.

PIECE BLOCKS: To make one block,
refer to the half-block piecing diagram,
top right. Sew an A piece to an H piece,
a B piece to a G piece, an A piece to a
G piece, a C piece to a G piece, and a
D piece to an E piece.

Sew the five units together. Add
piece F to complete the half-block.

In the same manner, assemble the
opposite half-block, using the reverse
pieces. Sew the two block halves together, matching seam lines carefully.

Piece 18 Prairie Pines blocks.

ASSEMBLE QUILT TOP: Referring
to the assembly diagram, *opposite, top*,
lay out the blocks on point with three
blocks across and four blocks down.
Place large setting triangles in the
openings around the outer edges.

Join the blocks in diagonal rows. Beginning with the top left row, join two
setting triangles with a tree block in the
center. To make the next row, join two

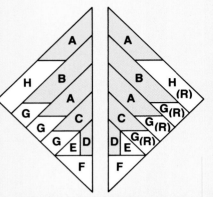

HALF-BLOCK PIECING DIAGRAM

setting triangles with three tree blocks
in the center. Continue in a similar
manner to form the rows.

Sew the rows together. Sew a corner
triangle to each corner of the quilt.
Trim excess triangles around the outer
edges, forming straight edges. After
trimming, the top should measure approximately 42¾x56½ inches, including seam allowances.

Sew a red border to a plaid border
along the long sides. Repeat for the
other borders.

Matching midpoints, stitch borders
to opposite sides of the quilt; trim.
Measure the quilt width. Trim the remaining two borders to this length.
Sew a border corner to each end of the
borders. Sew the borders to the top and
bottom of the quilt, matching seam
lines at corners.

FINISHING: Layer the quilt top, batting, and quilt backing; baste, working
out from the center. Quilt as desired.

From the remaining red fabric, cut
approximately eight yards of 2½-inch-
wide bias or straight-of-grain strips for
binding. Join the strips into one long
piece. Press the binding in half, *wrong*
sides facing, so it is 1¼ inches wide.

Matching the raw edges of the binding with the raw edges of the top, stitch
the binding around the quilt, mitering
the corners. Trim the excess quilt back
and batting. Bring the folded edge of
the binding to the quilt back; blindstitch in place.

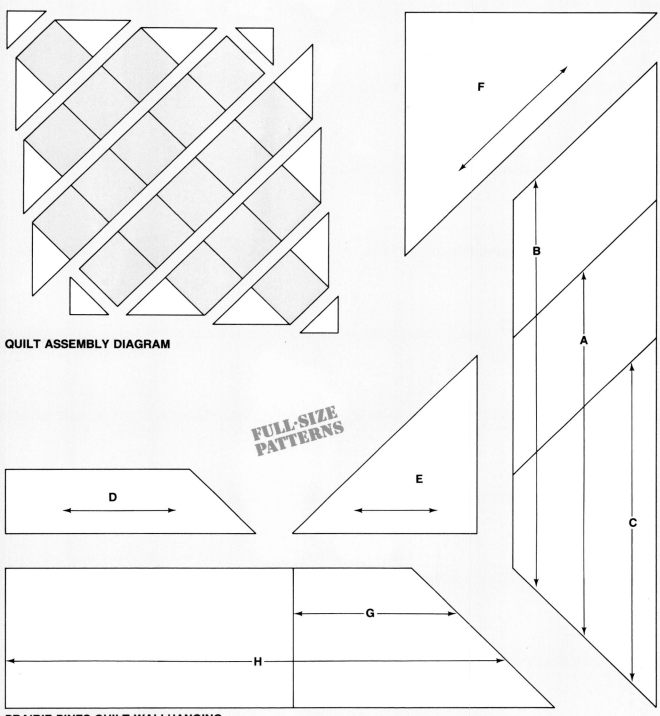

QUILT ASSEMBLY DIAGRAM

FULL·SIZE
PATTERNS

PRAIRIE PINES QUILT WALLHANGING

Hallelujah Chorus

Create a celestial choir to sing of the glory of the Christmas child. Begin with one angel that takes many forms when adapted to a variety of crafts. The angels in this section will help you make heavenly gifts for family and friends.

For stitching fun, use the chart on page 91 to cross-stitch the framed angel, *opposite, far left,* or to needlepoint the pillow behind it.

Set the angels amid white stars stitched from delicate fabrics and lace, and decorated with ribbon and tiny pearls. Star instructions are on page 94.

To decorate wooden ornaments, use the full-size painting pattern on page 92 for tracing. The enlarged pattern makes this dramatic door ornament, *right.*

A bustling Christmas workshop of pint-size Santa's helpers can turn out dozens of pierced-paper ornaments and glitter stars. All you need are the most basic materials and skills.

Pierced-paper ornaments require only heavy white paper, scissors, and two sizes of pins or needles. Simply trace the full-size patterns on page 93, then use the patterns to cut out the shapes. Pierce the paper through the indicated pinholes to create the illusion of beaded celestial robes.

A host of standing angels fills the wreaths *below* and *opposite, left.* Carrying candles of tiny stars, the angels stand among matching paper stars in two sizes.

The haloed trumpeting angel, *right,* is made in two pieces that are glued together under the wings. Add thread or ribbon hangers to make the heralding tree ornaments, *opposite.*

The standing angel is 5¼ inches high; the trumpeter is 5¾ inches.

The sparkling stars twinkling in the tree branches, *opposite,* are made with glue and glitter. The same free-hand technique can be used to make other fun ornament shapes.

Winged Sunbonnet Sues fly hither and yon amid the candles and baby's-breath on this country Christmas tree, *opposite.* A perennially favorite quilt motif, Sue is so easy to make that the whole family can participate in cutting and gluing a choir of little angels.

The full-size patterns on pages 96 and 97 include one for the cardboard base. The clothing, cut with pinking shears, is gathered and folded, then glued in place. The finished ornament is 7x9 inches.

A hearty trio of copper angels, mounted on a 9x16-inch painted board, is as easy to make as driving a nail. Hammering a nail into thin copper sheeting is all it takes to punch out the design on this plaque, *top right.* Coloring the angels with enamel paint is optional.

A few twists and tucks transform dried corn husks and tissue paper into a host of seraphim, *right.* The 4-inch-tall figures can trim a wreath, decorate a package, or dangle on a thread from a tree branch.

Instructions and patterns for the copper and corn-husk angels begin on page 94.

Painted Angel Wooden Ornament

Shown on pages 84 and 85.
Finished angel is 9 inches tall.

MATERIALS
6½x9-inch piece of ¼-inch-thick
  Baltic birch plywood
Jigsaw
Sandpaper
Acrylic paints and brushes
Graphite or carbon paper
Glue; spray varnish
Fine-point brown permanent marker
6 inches of nylon cording
8 crafts jewels for halo (optional)

INSTRUCTIONS
Using the full-size pattern on page 92,
transfer angel to plywood with graphite paper; cut out on jigsaw, and sand.
Drill a hole through halo for hanger.

Using photograph for color ideas,
paint with acrylic paints. When dry,
draw in face and other details with
marking pen. Glue crafts jewels onto
halo, if desired. Varnish; add hanger.

Door Ornament

Shown on page 85.
Finished angel is 20 inches tall.

MATERIALS
18x24-inch piece of ¼-inch Baltic
  birch plywood
Jigsaw
Sandpaper
Acrylic paints and brushes
Eight ½-inch-diameter crafts jewels
Fourteen ¼-inch-diameter crafts
  jewels
Graphite or carbon paper
Spray varnish
Hot-glue gun
6 inches of nylon cording
Fine-point brown permanent marker
Greens, ribbons, and silk flowers for
  embellishments (optional)

INSTRUCTIONS
Enlarge pattern on page 92. Follow
instructions for Painted Angel Wood-
en Ornament above. Paint scroll design on garment, if desired. Glue
evergreen to back of angel; glue silk
roses onto greens. Wire bow at base.

Needlepoint Angel Pillow

Shown on page 84.
*Finished pillow is 16x21½ inches
with ruffle.*

MATERIALS
16x22-inch piece of 10-mesh canvas
3-ply Paternayan Persian yarn in the
  following amounts and colors:
  63 yards of dark blue (511), 55
  yards of light blue (585), 42 yards
  of white (261), 18 yards of dark
  gray (222), 8 yards *each* of red
  (951) and gold (802), 5 yards of
  pink (905), 4 yards of yellow
  (704), 3 yards *each* of gray (212)
  and light gray (213), 2 yards *each*
  of tan (490) and flesh (494)
52 inches of ⅜-inch-diameter piping
⅔ yard of 60-inch-wide off-white
  wool fabric
Polyester fiberfill
Masking tape

INSTRUCTIONS
Bind canvas edges with masking tape.

STITCHING: Using two plies of yarn,
stitch outlines and small details in continental stitches, referring to the chart,
opposite. Work large areas and background in basket-weave stitches. (See
stitch diagrams on page 157.) When
graph is completed, add nine rows of
dark blue stitches on all sides for borders. Block finished needlepoint.

PILLOW ASSEMBLY: From white
wool, cut a 12x17-inch pillow back and
three 4x60-inch ruffle strips. Sew piping to pillow front, stitching close to
last row of needlepoint.

Using ½-inch seams, sew the ruffle
strips together end to end; sew ends
together. Machine-hem ruffle edge
with a ⅜-inch hem. Gather remaining
raw edge to fit around the pillow.

Sew ruffle to pillow front over piping stitch line. Pin pillow back over
pillow front (ruffles tucked inside). Using piping stitch line, sew pillow back
to front, leaving an opening for turning. Trim seams to within ½ inch. Turn
and stuff; sew opening closed.

Cross-Stitched Angel

Shown on page 84.
Finished design size is 5x8 inches.
Stitch count is 90 wide by 140 high.

MATERIALS
14x18-inch piece of light blue 18-
  count Aida fabric
Tapestry needle; embroidery hoop
One skein *each* of Anchor
  embroidery floss in the colors
  listed in the color key, *below*

INSTRUCTIONS
Find center of chart *opposite* and center
of fabric; begin stitching there. Using
two strands of floss, cross-stitch over
one thread. Frame as desired.

Glitter Stars

Shown on page 87.

MATERIALS
Glitter in assorted colors
Waxed paper
White crafts glue (use bottle with
  pointed tip)

INSTRUCTIONS
Lay waxed paper flat on work surface.
With pointed tip open on glue bottle,
draw star shapes on waxed paper.

Sprinkle glitter over stars, completely covering all glue. Let glue dry and
harden for 48 hours. Carefully peel
waxed paper away from star backs.

COLOR KEY (YARN/FLOSS)

■	No. 511/0851	Dark blue
◻	No. 585/0167	Light blue
☐	No. 261/0386	White
■	No. 951/035	Red
▨	No. 802/0304	Gold
▨	No. 905/040	Pink
☐	No. 704/0311	Yellow
■	No. 222/0401	Dark gray
◻	No. 212/0399	Gray
⊡	No. 213/398	Light gray
▨	No. 490/363	Tan
☐	No. 494/06	Flesh

**CROSS-STITCHED AND
NEEDLEPOINT ANGEL**

CROSS-STITCHED AND NEEDLEPOINT ANGEL

1 Square = 1 Stitch

PAINTED ANGEL ORNAMENT

ORNAMENT – Full-Size Pattern
DOOR ORNAMENT – 1 Square = 1 Inch

Pierced-Paper Angels and Stars

Shown on pages 86 and 87.

MATERIALS

Medium-weight watercolor paper
T-pin or large needle; straight pins
Small scissors; art knife
White glue; masking tape
Tracing paper
Foam pad or cardboard work surface

INSTRUCTIONS

Trace the full-size designs on this page. Tape tracing paper to watercolor paper to hold design in place.

Lay paper on work surface. With art knife, cut slits on trumpet angel's head; cut out spaces inside arms. Use T-pin to pierce holes marked by large dots and straight pins for smaller dots. With scissors, cut around outlines. Glue skirt behind angel wings on flying angel.

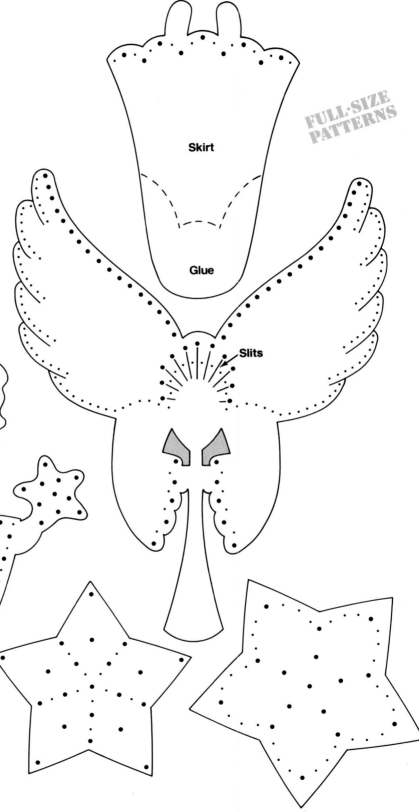

Skirt

Glue

Slits

PIERCED-PAPER ANGELS AND STARS

White Star Ornament

Shown on pages 84 and 85.
Finished star is 6 inches wide.

MATERIALS

Two 8-inch squares of linen, satin,
   dotted swiss, or cotton-blend fabric
Polyester fiberfill
¾ yard of white lace edging
White crafts flowers, beads, or lace
   appliqués (optional)
8 inches of ¼-inch-wide ribbon
Graph paper

INSTRUCTIONS

Enlarge pattern at *right* onto graph paper; cut out. Trace star onto one fabric piece (front).

Sew white lace edging around star front ¼ inch from raw edges. With right sides facing, sew other fabric square (back) to star front using lace stitching line. Leave an opening for turning. Clip corners; turn right side out. Stuff; sew opening closed. Stitch decoration (if desired) to front. Add a ribbon hanger.

Corn-Husk Angel

Shown on page 89.
Finished angel is 4 inches tall.

MATERIALS

To make one angel
1–2 ounces of dried corn husks
7½-inch square of tissue paper
3 inches of 19-gauge florist's wire
White or ecru quilting thread
Glycerin (for brittle shucks)
Crafts glue

INSTRUCTIONS

Before working with the corn husks, soak them in warm water for a few minutes, adding one or two drops of glycerin if the husks are thick or brittle. Keep the husks damp while working with them so they will be less apt to break. Before the husks are completely dry, bend the arms and wings into the desired positions.

HEAD: Following the grain, tear a husk along its length into a 1-inch-wide piece. Wad the tissue paper into a ball approximately ¾ inch in diameter.

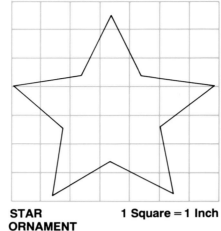

STAR ORNAMENT　　　　**1 Square = 1 Inch**

Twist the middle of the husk one complete turn. Place the tissue paper ball up tight against the twist. Fold both ends of the husk down over the ball, covering the ball and positioning the twist at the top. Twist the husks at the bottom of the ball, forming the neck. Tie the neck securely with quilting thread.

ARMS: Bend the ends of the wire to form small loops for the hands. Tear two strips of 1½-inch-wide husks. Fold one husk in half lengthwise and insert one loop end of the wire into the fold 1 inch from the end of the husk. The wire should be at a right angle to the husk. Fold the short end of the husk over the wire, covering the end. Wrap the longer end of the husk around the wire, ending at the middle of the wire as shown in Figure 1, *above right.* Tie the end securely.

Repeat to cover the other end of the wire, covering the wire completely.

To attach the arms to the head, separate the husks below the neck. Insert the arms between the husks. Holding the arms against the neck, wrap thread below the arms and crisscross around the neck. (See Figure 2, *right.*) Tie the thread securely.

SKIRT: Select four large husks for the skirt. Bend the angel's arms down, away from the head. Position the four husks around the angel's neck (two in front, two in back) so the narrow edges are at the neck and the wide edges go up over her head. Tie the husks securely around the angel's neck.

Bend the arms back up through the side slits. Carefully fold the husks down, forming the skirt and exposing the angel's head.

BODICE: Gather the skirt at the angel's waist, overlapping the side edges. Form the bodice by tying thread securely around the angel's waist and crisscrossing the thread around the angel's shoulders. Tie thread securely.

WINGS: Trace the wing pattern, *below.* Choose a large coarse husk for the wings. Fold the husk in half widthwise, across the grain. Lay the pattern on the husk, following the grain as indicated on the pattern. Cut out the wing; unfold. Glue wing to back of the bodice.

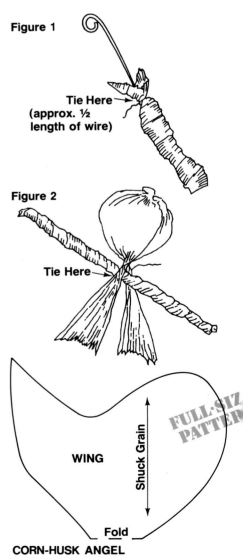

Figure 1

Tie Here
(approx. ½
length of wire)

Figure 2

Tie Here

WING

Shuck Grain

FULL-SIZE PATTERN

Fold

CORN-HUSK ANGEL

Copper Angel Plaque

Shown on page 89.
Finished plaque is 9x16 inches.

MATERIALS

7x14-inch sheet of 36-gauge copper
9x16-inch piece of 1-inch pine
Hammer and large nail or ice pick
Masking tape
Newspapers; paper towels
Mat acrylic medium
Tube of black acrylic paint
Paintbrushes; turpentine
Red, black, green, peach, and cream
    enamel paints
Latex or acrylic dark green paint for
    wood base
Fine steel wool
Copper tacks or nails
Clear acrylic spray
Tracing paper and pencil

INSTRUCTIONS

Trace the angel pattern, *right,* expanding the design so there are three angels separated by two hearts.

Securely tape the copper to the pine. Tape paper pattern over copper.

Punch the design with a hammer and an ice pick or a nail. Punch slightly larger holes for the eyes and mouth; remove paper pattern. Remove any tape residue with lighter fluid.

ANTIQUING: Prepare an antiquing solution by stirring together 2 tablespoons of acrylic medium, one-third of the tube of black acrylic paint, and a few drops of water in a glass jar.

Place the copper on newspaper. Generously spread the antiquing solution on the copper, working it into the holes. Wipe off the solution with a paper towel until the copper is clean but antiquing residue is left in the holes. If the solution becomes too dry to wipe off easily, dampen the paper towel.

Lightly buff the copper surface with steel wool; wipe the surface clean with a soft rag or paper towel. To help prevent the copper from tarnishing, spray the surface evenly with clear acrylic spray; let dry completely.

PAINTING: Paint the design, taking care not to get paint in the holes. If necessary, remove paint with turpentine and repaint as needed.

continued

COPPER ANGEL PLAQUE

Use peach paint for the faces, hands, and feet. Use cream paint on wings, collars, petticoats, and bloomers.

Using the black enamel, tint the red and green enamel paints for deeper shades. Paint the dresses green. Paint the bows and hearts red.

Let the paint dry at least five days. This is important to achieve a hard finish that will resist scratches and other damage.

FINISHING: Sand the wooden base; paint with dark green paint. Secure copper to base with copper tacks or nails spaced 2 inches apart.

To store the plaque, cover it loosely with tissue paper or cloth; do not store or wrap the plaque in plastic.

Sunbonnet Sue Angel Ornament

Shown on page 88.
Finished ornament is 7x9 inches.

MATERIALS

⅛ yard *each* of 45-inch-wide tan print
    and light green print fabrics
4 inches of ⅛-inch-wide ribbon
10 inches of 1-inch-wide ecru
    gathered eyelet
2½x8-inch piece of heavyweight
    watercolor paper
5½x9-inch piece of white cardboard
White glue
Pinking shears
Tracing paper and pencil
Powdered blush

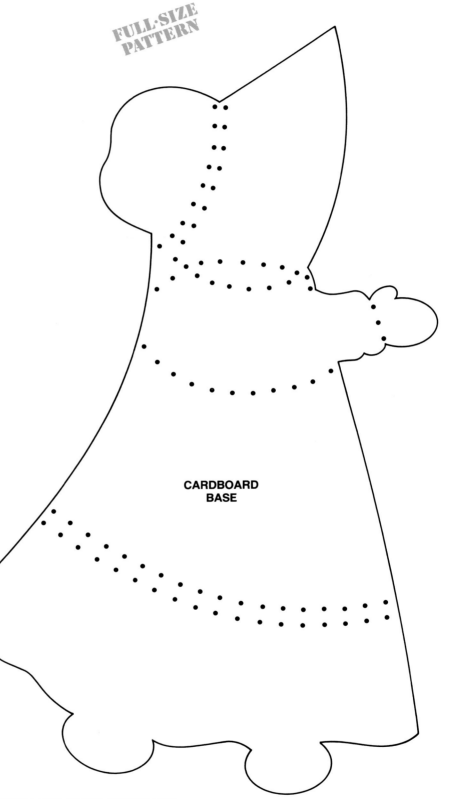

FULL-SIZE PATTERN

CARDBOARD BASE

SUNBONNET SUE ANGEL ORNAMENT

INSTRUCTIONS

Trace the patterns, *opposite* and *below.* Cut base shape from cardboard and the wings from watercolor paper. Pin all clothing patterns to fabrics; cut out with pinking shears.

Note: All fabric gathering is done with one row of machine stitching.

Gather top edge of skirt ruffle; glue top and side edges in place on cardboard shape. Glue a 4½-inch length of eyelet in place above skirt ruffle.

Gather top edge of apron. Lay apron atop cardboard, adjusting as necessary to allow ¾ inch of eyelet to show; glue top and side edges.

Glue edges of bonnet cap in place, allowing bonnet to puff out at center. Repeat for bonnet brim. Cover joined bonnet edges with 2 inches of ribbon.

Gather sleeve cap and wrist to fit cardboard outline. Glue the gathered edge of a 4-inch length of eyelet under the sleeve edge, tapering it from underarm to just above the wrist. Glue sleeve edges in place, letting sleeve puff out at center.

Fold wings along fold line; tint the outside edges pink with powdered blush. Glue folded edge of wing to the back of the ornament at the shoulder. Add a ribbon bow.

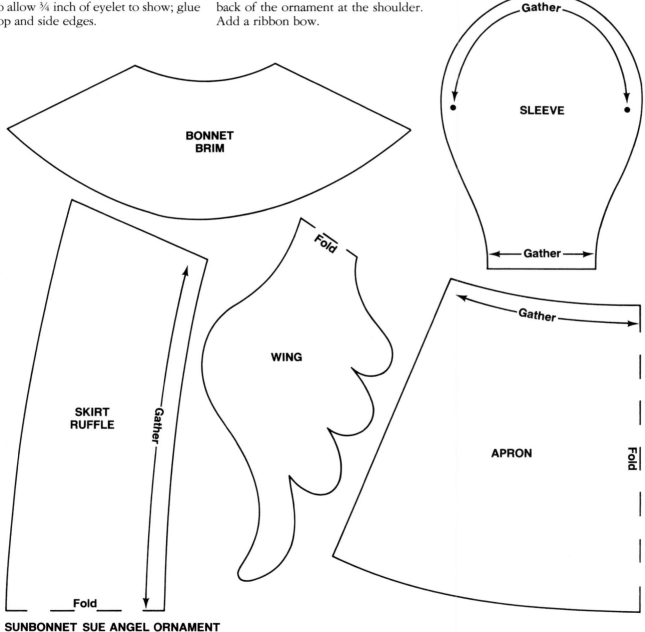

FULL-SIZE PATTERNS

BONNET CAP

SLEEVE

Gather

Gather

BONNET BRIM

WING

Fold

SKIRT RUFFLE

Gather

Fold

Gather

APRON

Fold

SUNBONNET SUE ANGEL ORNAMENT

Christmas in the Heart of Country

Barn red and forest green guarantee a true down-home holiday. Here they're found on primitive wood shapes. The next four pages are full of country colors on quilts, afghans, and toys.

The stenciled wood blocks, *opposite,* convey happy season's greetings. The folk-art heart that can stand atop each block adds love to a cheery message.

Two tree-toting Santas, large and small, also are crafted from painted wood.

Dried apple ornaments and wreaths, splashed with cinnamon fragrance, add a natural touch to an indoor tree, *right.*

Instructions begin on page 106.

Give those who are dear to your heart a Christmas full of country spirit with gifts that say they were made in America, with love.

This elfin Santa, *left*, is a 23-inch doll dressed in warm winter underwear, stockings, and scratchy red woolen pants with suspenders. Heavy black florist's wire easily bends into spectacles to perch merrily over his twinkly button eyes.

You'll achieve an antique look if you tea-dye red and white striped fabrics for Santa's shirt and stockings. Just soak the fabric in ordinary tea for a few minutes; when dry, the fabric will have the weathered look of yesteryear.

The red of poinsettias and the green of fragrant pine nestle in a frame of snowlike white in each block of this traditional crocheted granny-square afghan, *opposite*.

The basic motif is worked in just five rounds of single and double crochet stitches. Join 204 motifs and add a lacy edging to complete this 50x70-inch afghan.

Directions for the afghan and the Santa begin on page 109.

Nothing chases away the chill of a winter evening like snuggling down under a warm quilt or afghan beside the glowing old stove.

Weave a diamond pattern of rich red crocheted strands through the snowy field of this easy-to-stitch crocheted afghan, *below.*

A mesh background of double crochet stitches provides the foundation for weaving the strands under and over to form a diamond pattern. Luxurious fringe completes the 45x63-inch afghan.

Like the star that led the magi to Bethlehem, a constellation of red and green stars shines brightly on this Mariner's Compass pieced and appliquéd quilt, *opposite.* This pattern is a bit complex, but careful sewing is the key to its success.

The large patchwork star, or compass, is appliquéd onto the background fabric. Red stars in the corners complete each block. Joining nine blocks with a star-studded border and simple outline quilting finishes the 84-inch-square quilt.

A technique called needle-rolling, suggested for appliquéing the small stars onto the quilt background, is explained on page 112.

Full-size patterns and instructions begin on page 111.

For Christmas dinner by candlelight, borrow a tabletop idea from the Scandinavians. This star-topped and painted candlestand, *above,* is made by cutting two trees from plywood and locking them together along complementary slots cut into the center of each tree.

Light up the 13¼-inch-tall tree with 12 flickering candles; set it by the window to bid a cheerful welcome to nighttime passersby.

One of the miracles of Christmas is the ordinary green succulent plant that blossoms with bright yellow-orange flowers just in time for the holidays. These exotic blooms are re-created in this bold appliquéd Christmas Cactus quilt, *opposite.*

A patchwork of red, green, and gold outlines the four appliquéd blocks that form the center of this 84-inch-square quilt. The quilt's striking graphic design makes it a standout on a bed or proudly displayed as a wall hanging.

Full-size patterns and instructions are on pages 116 and 117.

Dried Apple Ornaments

Shown on page 99.

MATERIALS

To make two ornaments
Two large dried apple slices
½ yard of ⅝-inch-wide plaid taffeta ribbon
22-gauge florist's wire
Two preserved leatherleaf ferns
Two red globe amaranth flowers or other decorations
Crafts glue or hot-glue gun
Clear spray sealer
Oil of cinnamon
Sharp scissors

INSTRUCTIONS

Carefully slit the ribbon in half. From each length of ribbon, cut a 4-inch-long piece. Glue a ribbon piece to the back of each apple slice, forming ornament hangers.

Tie each of the remaining ribbon pieces into a bow, securing the bows with florist's wire.

Using the hot-glue gun, glue two short leaflets of the fern on the front of one apple slice. Glue a bow in front of the fern, then glue a flower in the center of the bow. Repeat to make the second ornament.

Spray front and back of ornaments with clear sealer. Add a few drops of cinnamon oil to the back. To prolong the life of the ornaments, protect them from excessive humidity.

Dried Apple Wreath

Shown on page 99.
Finished wreaths are approximately 4 inches in diameter.

MATERIALS

To make one wreath
Purchased dried apple slices
4-inch-diameter vine wreath
1 yard of ⅝-inch-wide plaid ribbon
20-gauge green florist's wire
Clear spray sealer
Oil of cinnamon
Hot-glue gun
Wire cutter
Sharp scissors

INSTRUCTIONS

Select dried apple slices of uniform size for the wreath. If the slices are dry and brittle, moisten them *slightly* to work with them. Before working with each piece, it is helpful to press it between your palms for several seconds before gently stretching and bending it.

Position the first piece at the top of the wreath. Glue the slices around the wreath, overlapping them in a consistent direction. Overlap the last piece over both the previous slice and the beginning piece. Allow time for the glue to set as you add each slice.

Spray the wreath with clear sealer.

Form a small hanging loop at the back of the wreath from florist's wire. Add a few drops of cinnamon oil to the back of the wreath.

Tie the ribbon into a bow; glue it to the wreath, covering the irregular area at the top of the wreath.

To prolong the life of the wreath, protect it from excessive humidity.

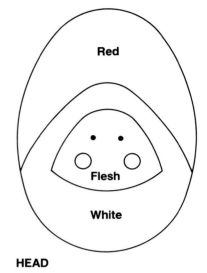

HEAD

FULL-SIZE PATTERNS

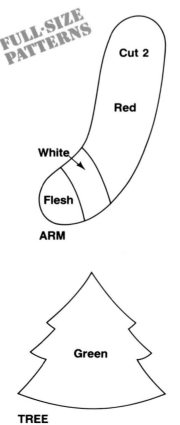

ARM

TREE
SMALL WOODEN SANTA DOLL

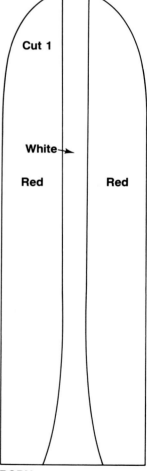

BODY

Wooden Santa Dolls

Shown on pages 98 and 99.
Large Santa is 13 inches tall; small
Santa is 7½ inches tall.

MATERIALS

■ For both Santas

Band saw and router
Drill and drill bits
Spanish moss for hair
Raw spinning wool for beard
Tracing paper and pencil
Graphite or carbon paper
Acrylic paints in the following colors:
    red, green, white, flesh, black,
    ivory, and rust
Antiquing mud
Paint thinner
Paintbrushes
Sandpaper; steel wool
Mat-finish clear acrylic spray
Hot-glue gun

■ For the large Santa

4x2¾-inch wooden egg for head
9-inch-long piece of 3½-inch-
    diameter wooden post for body
3-inch-long piece of ½-inch-diameter
    wooden dowel
1-inch-long piece of 3/16-inch-diameter
    wooden dowel for trunk
3-inch square of ½-inch pine for tree
1x4x6-inch piece of pine for arms
3½x2¾x4-inch oval basket
Three ¾-inch wooden apples or
    cherries
Four 1- to 1½-inch-long pinecones
Twig approximately 8 inches long
    and ¼ inch in diameter for staff
Two 14-mm bells
3-inch-diameter grapevine wreath
One red and two dark green 8-inch-
    long strands of embroidery floss
Two 1¼-inch-long wire nails

■ For the small Santa

2x1¾-inch wooden egg for head
5½-inch-long piece of wooden
    handrail for body
2-inch-long piece of ¼-inch-diameter
    wooden dowel
¾-inch-long piece of ⅛-inch-diameter
    wooden dowel for trunk
3-inch square of ⅜-inch birch
    plywood for arms
2-inch square of ¼-inch birch
    plywood for tree
3-inch-tall round basket

Three ½-inch wooden apples
Four ½- to 1-inch-long pinecones
Twig approximately 6 inches long
    and ⅛ inch in diameter for staff
Two 11-mm bells
2-inch-diameter grapevine wreath
One red and two dark green 6-inch-
    long strands of embroidery floss
⅞-inch-long wire nails

INSTRUCTIONS

Trace the full-size Santa patterns onto tracing paper. The patterns for the small Santa are *opposite;* patterns for the large Santa are *below* and on page 108. Using graphite or carbon paper, transfer the arm and tree patterns to the appropriate wood pieces.

Use a band saw to cut out the pieces, then taper the top of each arm to make it thinner where it will join the body. Rout around the tapered side of the arms and around the trees.

Referring to the body pattern as a guide, round the top of the body piece.

Drill a hole to fit the larger dowel in the bottom center of the fat end of the egg. Glue the larger dowel in the egg. Using the same drill bit, drill a hole in the top of the body. Drill a hole to fit the tree trunk dowel in the bottom of the tree. Glue the trunk in the tree. Using the same drill bit, drill a hole in the left hand to hold the tree trunk.

Using a drill bit slightly larger than the diameter of the stick, drill a hole for the staff through the right hand.

Sand all wooden pieces. Referring to the patterns for colors, paint the pieces. Do not paint eyes and cheeks at this time. To give the pieces a worn look, lightly sand some paint off in various areas.

Mix the antiquing mud with paint thinner to achieve a consistency for brushing. Brush on the antiquing mixture; let dry at least 5 minutes. Wipe off the excess with paper towels. Buff random areas with steel wool to remove some of the antiquing. Paint eyes black; mix ivory and rust to paint the cheeks; let dry. Spray all pieces with acrylic spray.

Nail the arms to the body. Glue the head to the body.

To clean the wool for the beard, soak the wool in tepid water to which a few drops of liquid dish soap have been added; rinse in clear water. Let dry; carefully comb the wool. Glue the wool to Santa's face, forming a beard and mustache. Glue moss around the face, forming the hair.

Fill the basket with moss. Glue apples and pinecones in the moss at the top of the basket. Slip the basket on Santa's right arm. Slip the staff through the hole in the right hand.

Twist the strands of embroidery floss together. Tie each end to one bell. Wrap the bells around the wreath. Slip the wreath on Santa's left arm. Insert the tree in the hole, holding the wreath in place.

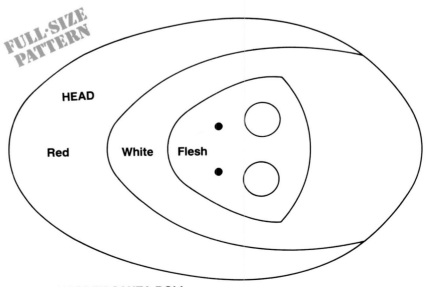

LARGE WOODEN SANTA DOLL

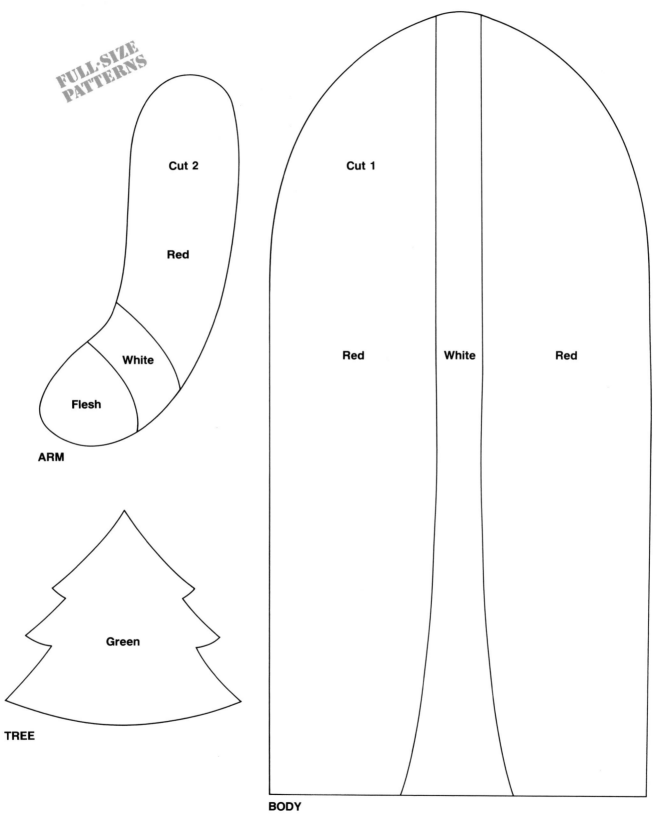

FULL-SIZE PATTERNS

Cut 2

Red

White

Flesh

ARM

Green

TREE

Cut 1

Red

White

Red

BODY

LARGE WOODEN SANTA DOLL

Holiday Blocks

Shown on page 98.
Finished blocks are 8 to 19 inches long.

MATERIALS

■ For all blocks
Band saw and router
Drill and drill bits
Red, green, and white acrylic crafts
    paints
Wood glue
Paintbrushes
Antiquing mud
Paint thinner
Mat-finish clear acrylic spray
Stencil brush
2-inch-tall purchased letter stencils
Medium sandpaper; steel wool
Graphite or carbon paper

■ For Joy block
4x4x8-inch wood block
Two 4-inch-tall candles
6½-inch-long piece of ¼-inch-
    diameter wooden dowel
2x4x4-inch piece of wood for heart

■ For Noel block
4x4x9¾-inch wood block
Four 4-inch-tall candles
5½-inch-long piece of ¼-inch-
    diameter wooden dowel
2x4x4-inch piece of wood for heart

■ For Merry Christmas blocks
4x4x12½-inch wood block
4x4x19-inch wood block
4½-inch-long piece of ¼-inch-
    diameter wooden dowel
2x4x4-inch piece of wood for heart

INSTRUCTIONS
Trace the heart pattern, *above right.* For the Joy, Noel, and Merry blocks, use graphite or carbon paper to transfer the heart outline to the 2x4x4-inch pieces of wood. Using a band saw, cut out the hearts. Rout the heart edges.

In each of the blocks *except* the Christmas block, drill a ¼-inch-diameter hole approximately 1 inch deep for a dowel in the center top of the block. On the Joy block, use the appropriate size of bit to drill a 1-inch-deep hole for a candle 1½ inches from each end of the block. In a similar manner, drill

FULL-SIZE PATTERN

HOLIDAY BLOCKS HEART

holes for candles approximately 1½ inches and 3⅛ inches from each end of the Noel block.

Sand the hearts and the 4x4-inch blocks of wood. Paint the Noel, Joy, and Merry blocks green. Paint the hearts and the Christmas block red.

Using a stencil brush and white paint, stencil the appropriate letters on each block; let dry.

Thin the antiquing mud with paint thinner so it will spread on easily. Brush the antiquing solution on the blocks, hearts, and dowels; let dry 5 minutes or longer for a deeper color. Using paper towels, wipe off the excess solution. To give the blocks and hearts an aged appearance, rub the pieces lightly with steel wool to remove some of the paint. Spray all the pieces with acrylic spray.

Glue a heart onto the top of each dowel. Insert the dowels and candles in the drilled holes in each block. If the bottoms of the dowels with the hearts are not glued in the blocks, the dowels can be removed to make out-of-season storage easier.

Poinsettia Afghan

Shown on page 101.
Finished size is 50x70 inches.

MATERIALS
Coats & Clark Red Heart 4-ply knit
    and crochet yarn (3.5-ounce
    skein): 7 skeins of color A,
    cardinal (917); 3 skeins of color B,
    paddy green (686); 8 skeins of
    color C, off-white (003)
Size J crochet hook or size to obtain
    gauge given below
Tapestry needle

Abbreviations: See page 35.
Gauge: Each motif is 4 inches
    square.

INSTRUCTIONS
POINSETTIA MOTIF: (Make 204.)

With crochet hook and color A, ch 6, join with sl st to form a ring.

Rnd 1: Ch 5 (counts as 1 dc and ch 2), (dc into ring, ch 2) 7 times, sl st to third ch of beg ch-5—8 ch-2 spaces.

Rnd 2: Sl st in next ch-2 sp; **ch 3, holding back last lp of each dc, work 3 dc in next ch-2 sp; yo, draw through all lps on hook—beg cl made;** (**ch 5, holding back last lp of each dc, work 4 dc tog into next sp, yo, draw through all lps on hook— cl made**) 7 times; ch 5, join with sl st to top of beg cl; fasten off.

continued

Rnd 3: Using color B, join yarn into top of first cl; ch 1, sc into same st, * ch 2, working over the ch-5 arch so as to enclose it, work 1 dc into next dc of first rnd, ch 2, sc into top of next cl; rep from *, omitting sc at end; join last ch-2 with sl st to first sc; fasten off.

Rnd 4: Using color C, sl st into next ch, ch 1, sc into same ch; * ch 3, sc into next sp; rep from * around omitting sc at end; join last ch-3 with sl st to first sc.

Rnd 5: Sl st into next ch-3 lp, ch 3 (count as 1 dc); in same lp work dc, ch 2, and 2 dc; * ch 2, sc into next ch-3 lp, (ch 3, sc into next ch-3 lp) 2 times; ch 2 **; 2 dc, ch 2, and 2 dc into next ch-3 lp—corner made; rep from * twice more; then rep from * to **; join with sl st to top of beg ch-3; fasten off.

FINISHING: With color C, and stitching through the back lps on each motif, whipstitch the motifs together making 17 rows of 12 motifs each.

BORDER: *Rnd 1:* With color C, sc around afghan working sc in each sc and dc around and working 2 sc in each ch-2 lp and 3 sc in each ch-3 lp; in each ch-2 corner sp, work sc, ch 2, and sc; join with sl st to first sc.

Rnd 2: Ch 7, dc in fourth ch from hook; then make dc in the same sc where the ch-7 began; * sk 3 sc, dc in next sc, ch 4, dc in fourth ch from hook, dc in same sc where ch-4 began; rep from * around, making an extra pattern repeat at corners in ch-2 sp.

Weave in the ends and block.

All-American Santa
Shown on page 100.
Finished Santa is 23 inches tall.

MATERIALS
1 yard of muslin for doll body
½ yard of narrow red/white striped knit fabric for shirt
⅓ yard of wide red/white striped knit fabric for stockings
½ yard of red wool for pants, hat
⅛ yard of gray fabric for suspenders
2¼x16-inch strip of white fake fur
Reynolds Nuance (50-gram ball)—
    one skein of white (584) for hair
Large-eyed needle

Two ½-inch-diameter black buttons for eyes
Six ¾-inch-diameter buttons for shirt and suspenders
Polyester fiberfill
Scrap of polyester batting
Carpet thread
17 inches of heavy black florist's wire for glasses
Needle-nose pliers
Graph paper and pencil

INSTRUCTIONS
Enlarge the patterns, *opposite,* onto graph paper. Referring to the materials list, cut pieces from appropriate fabrics. From the wide striped fabric, cut four foot/stocking pieces ⅛ *inch larger* all around than the pattern.

Note: Stitch all pieces with right sides facing, taking ¼-inch seam allowances unless directed otherwise.

BODY: For the head, sew the ear fronts to the ear backs, leaving the straight sides open. Turn, stuff lightly, and sew the raw edges to the head front between the markings.

Sew the head back to the head front, keeping the ears inside and leaving an opening at the neck for turning. Turn, stuff firmly, sew closed.

Turn under the edge of the nose piece. Place the nose over the face at the markings; whipstitch the nose to the face, stuffing as you sew.

Sew the two body back pieces together along center seam, leaving an opening for stuffing. Repeat for front.

On the body front, baste batting to the wrong sides of the hands.

Sew the body front to the body back around the perimeter, leaving the leg bottoms open. Turn the raw edges of the leg bottoms under ¼ inch, and machine-baste; leave long threads hanging. Machine-topstitch finger lines on the hands.

Sew two foot pieces together for each leg, leaving the tops open. Stuff feet firmly. Insert feet into leg openings of body with seams centered and feet pointing forward. Draw the leg threads snugly around the inserted feet tops; tie, then hand-stitch feet to legs.

Stuff the body firmly; sew closed. Do not sew the head to the body until the shirt is on the body.

SHIRT: Sew a seam ½ inch from the fold on the shirt front, forming a false shirt placket; press flat.

Sew the shirt front to the shirt back at the shoulders; do not leave a neck opening. Hem the sleeves. Sew the sleeves to the shirt, matching the center top of the sleeve to the shoulder seam. Sew the underarm and shirt side seams in one long seam.

Put shirt on doll. Sew four buttons on placket, spaced 1 inch apart.

HAIR: Using carpet thread, securely sew the head to the body.

For the beard, eyebrows, and mustache, pull double strands of yarn (one stitch at a time) along the stitch lines, leaving 8-inch yarn lengths for the beard, 1-inch lengths for the mustache, and ½-inch lengths for the eyebrows.

For Santa's balding head, fill in a hairline from ear to ear on the back of the head. Make 3-inch hair lengths, work three rows of hair. Trim the yarn.

Sew buttons in place for the eyes.

PANTS: Join two pants pieces at the inseam; repeat for the two remaining pieces. Press the inseams. Sew pants together along the center front/center back crotch seam. Sew the side seams. Turn the pants right side out.

Zigzag-stitch raw edges of the waistband and leg bottoms. Turn waistband and leg bottom edges under 1 inch.

On the waistband, topstitch ½ inch from folds; topstitch a second row ¼ inch below first row.

Topstitch the hems on the leg bottoms; add a second row of stitching ¼ inch from the first rows.

For the suspenders, sew two pieces together, leaving an opening for turning along one edge of strap; repeat for the second pair. Turn right side out; press and topstitch ¼ inch from edges.

Put the pants on the doll; sew the suspenders to the pants, fitting them to doll. Sew on the suspender buttons.

STOCKINGS: Sew two of the stocking pieces together, leaving the tops open. Repeat for second stocking.

HAT: Sew the hat front to the hat back, leaving the bottom edge open.

From the white fake fur, cut a 2¼x13-inch hat-trim rectangle. Sew

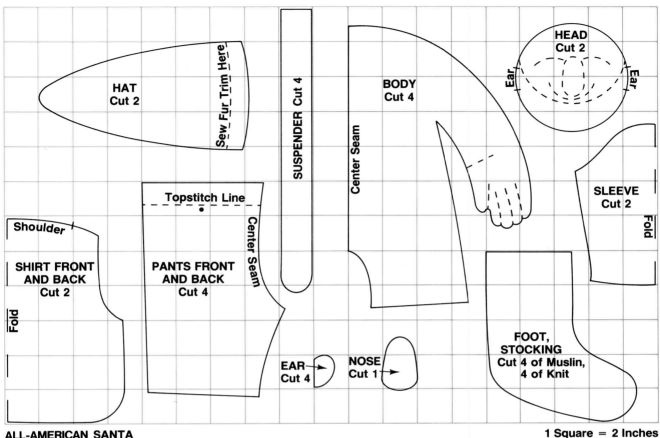

ALL-AMERICAN SANTA

1 Square = 2 Inches

the ends together. With raw edges together, sew the right side of the fur trim inside the hat bottom. Turn the trim to the right side on the outside of the hat bottom. Referring to the pattern, turn the raw edge under and sew along the trim line.

Cut a 2¼-inch-diameter circle for the hat-point trim. Hand-baste around the circle; gather the threads tightly to pull the circle into a ball. Hand-sew the ball to the hat point, drawing the raw edges inside to hide them.

GLASSES: Cut two 3-inch pieces and one 11-inch piece of wire. At the center of the long wire, bend 1½ inches around the nose to form the bridge. Bend the two 3-inch wires into lenses with 1½-inch bottom edges and two ¾-inch sides; twist the ends tightly around the long wire at the sides of the bridge to complete the lenses. Bend the long wire at the corners of lenses back toward the ears; bend the ends around the ears.

Mariner's Compass Quilt

Shown on page 103.
Finished quilt is 84 inches square.
Finished block is 24 inches square.

MATERIALS
8 yards of muslin fabric
2¾ yards of green print fabric
2½ yards of red print fabric
1½ yards of gold print fabric
5 yards of backing fabric
Cardboard or plastic for templates
Quilt batting

INSTRUCTIONS
Trace the full-size patterns on page 113. Make a template from cardboard or plastic for each pattern piece. The patterns are finished size; add ¼-inch seam allowances to all pieces when cutting them from fabric.

CUTTING: From the muslin fabric, cut nine 24½-inch squares down the length of the yardage. From the fabric that is left at the side, cut four border strips 6½x86 inches. Measurements for the squares and borders include ¼-inch seam allowances. Measurements for borders are longer than is needed; trim the borders to the length needed after the blocks are assembled.

From the remaining muslin fabric, cut 288 A pieces.

From the red print fabric, cut nine E octagons, 72 C wedges, and 60 F stars. Mark the F stars on the *right* side of the fabric; use the marking as the turn-under line when appliquéing the pieces onto the muslin. When cutting the F stars, leave only a generous ⅛-inch seam allowance to reduce bulk on the tight curves and sharp points.

From the green print fabric, cut 72 D wedges and 24 F stars.

From the gold print fabric, cut 144 B wedges.

continued

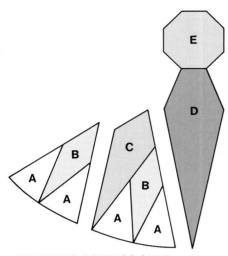

MARINER'S COMPASS QUILT PIECING DIAGRAM

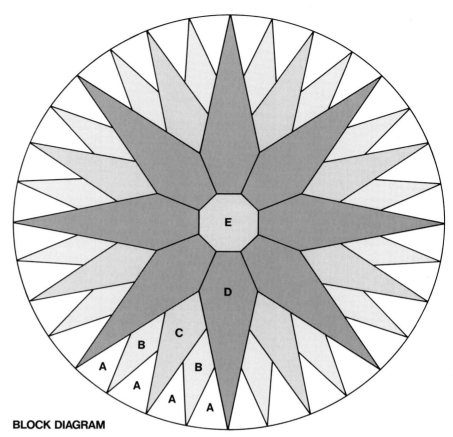

BLOCK DIAGRAM

PIECING: Referring to the piecing diagram, *above,* piece eight sections for the compass. To make one section, sew an A wedge to each side of a B piece; make two AB units for each section. Sew an AB unit to each side of a C piece. Sew the ABC unit to one side of a D piece. Sew the top of the D piece to one side of an E octagon. Join the successive ABC sections to the center E octagon and to the side of the previous ABC section.

When compass is complete, baste under ¼ inch around the outer edge of the circle.

Fold one large muslin square in half horizontally, vertically, and diagonally; crease folds to create placement guidelines for the compass. Center the compass on the block; appliqué compass to the square. To reduce bulk, work from the back side and carefully cut away the muslin behind the compass, leaving a ¼-inch seam allowance.

Appliqué a red F star in each corner of the block. Use matching thread and roll under the seam allowance around the star.

Make nine blocks.

ASSEMBLY: Join completed blocks in three rows with three blocks in each row. Join the rows; press.

continued

Needle-Rolling Appliqué

Some appliqué shapes, such as the Mariner's Compass stars and Christmas Cactus leaves, have very tight curves. Traditional ¼-inch seam allowances are impossible to manage in such cases. By using this technique to stitch such designs, you'll get excellent results—and be able to appliqué other intricate designs.

Begin by tracing around the appliqué shape (the star, for example) onto the *right* side of the fabric. This drawn line is the *sewing* line. Cut out the shape, adding *only ⅛ inch* all around for seams.

Next, using the pattern template and a water-erasable pen, mark placement lines for the motif on background fabric.

Pin the appliqués to the background, carefully matching the sewing line on each appliqué piece to the placement lines on the background fabric.

Using your fingertips and the tip of the needle, pinch and roll under a small section of the seam allowance on the appliqué shape, adjusting the position of the folded edge so it covers the placement line on the background fabric. Pin the appliqué in place as needed.

Next, sew each appliqué in place. As you stitch, continue using the tip of the needle to tuck under the seam allowance along the drawn line and match it to the placement line. Use sharp, small scissors to clip the curves as needed.

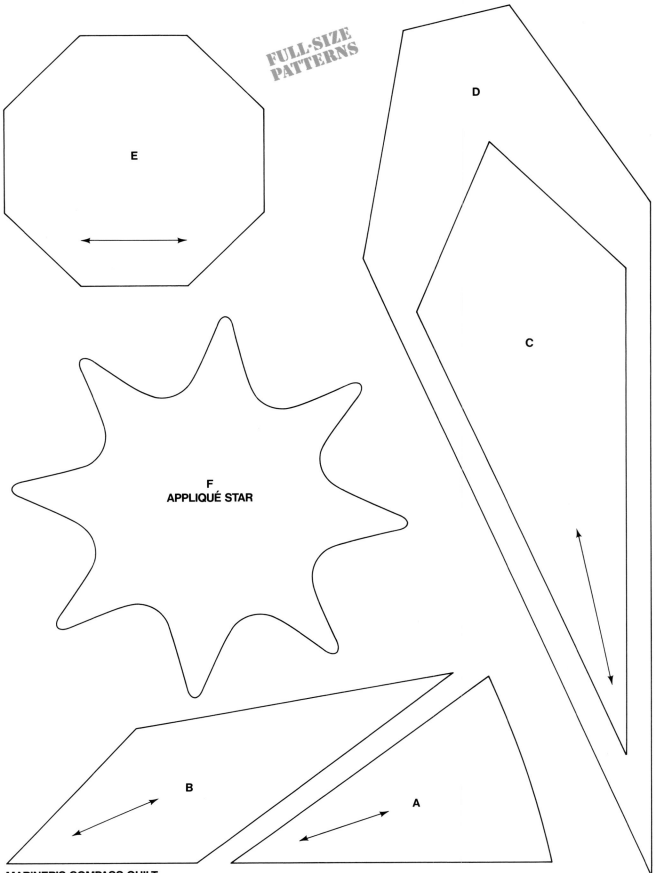

FULL-SIZE PATTERNS

E

D

C

F
APPLIQUÉ STAR

B

A

MARINER'S COMPASS QUILT

113

Measure the quilt top; cut two borders this length (approximately 72½ inches, including seam allowances). Appliqué six green and five red F stars to *each* trimmed border, leaving approximately 2½ to 3 inches of space between the stars. Sew the borders to opposite sides of the quilt top; press.

Measure the quilt, including the borders. Cut the remaining two borders this length (approximately 84½ inches, including seam allowances). Appliqué seven red and six green F stars to *each* border. Sew these borders to the remaining sides of the quilt top.

FINISHING: Cut the backing fabric into two 2½-yard lengths. Cut one length in half lengthwise. Matching selvage edges, sew a narrow panel to each side of the full panel. Trim the seam allowances to ¼ inch.

Layer and baste the quilt back, batting, and quilt top. Quilt as desired.

From the remaining red fabric, cut 10½ to 11 yards of 2¼-inch-wide bias or straight-grain strips for the binding. Press the binding in half with wrong sides facing so it is 1⅛ inches wide.

Match the raw edges of the binding with the raw edge of the quilt. Stitch the binding to the quilt, mitering corners. Trim excess backing and batting. Turn the folded edge of the binding to the quilt back; blindstitch in place.

Diamond-Weave Crocheted Afghan

Shown on page 102.
Finished afghan, excluding fringe, measures 45x63 inches.

MATERIALS

Coats & Clark Red Heart (R) "Super Saver" 4-ply yarn (8-ounce skein):
5 skeins of aran (313) and
3 skeins of burgundy (376)
Size H crochet hook or size to obtain gauge cited below
Yarn needle

Abbreviations: See page 35.
Gauge: In mesh background: 2 sps = 1 inch; 6 rows = 3½ inches.

INSTRUCTIONS

■ For the mesh background

Starting at bottom with aran, ch 186, having 4 ch sts to 1 inch.

Row 1: Dc in sixth ch from hook—starting sp made; * ch 1, sk next ch, dc in next ch—sp made; rep from * across—91 sps; ch 4, turn.

Row 2: Sk first dc, dc in next dc—starting sp over sp made; * ch 1, dc in next dc—sp over sp made; rep from * across; end with ch 1, sk first ch of turning-ch, dc in next ch—91 sps; ch 4, turn.

Row 3: Make 6 sps, * holding back on hook the last lp of each dc, make 2 dc in next sp, yo and draw through all 3 lps on hook, dc in next dc—bl over sp made; make 12 sps; rep from * across; end with 6 sps; ch 4, turn.

Row 4: Make 5 sps, * 1 bl, ch 1, dc in last dc of next block—sp over bl made; 1 bl, 10 sps; rep from * across; end with 5 sps; ch 4, turn.

Row 5: Make 4 sps, * 1 bl, 3 sps, 1 bl, 8 sps; rep from * across; end with 4 sps; ch 4, turn.

Row 6: Make 3 sps, * (1 bl, 2 sps) twice; 1 bl, 6 sps; rep from * across; end with 3 sps; ch 4, turn.

Row 7: Make 2 sps, * 1 bl, 2 sps, 1 bl, 1 sp, 1 bl, 2 sps, 1 bl, 4 sps; rep from * across; end with 2 sps; ch 4, turn.

Row 8: Make 1 sp, * 1 bl, 2 sps, 1 bl, 3 sps, (1 bl, 2 sps) twice; rep from * across; end with 1 sp; ch 3, turn.

Row 9: Make 1 bl, * 2 sps, 1 bl, 5 sps, 1 bl, 2 sps, 2 bls; rep from * across, end with a bl; ch 4, turn.

Row 10: Make 2 sps, * 1 bl, 7 sps, 1 bl, 4 sps. Rep from * across, end with 2 sps; ch 4, turn.

Row 11: Make 1 sp, * 1 bl, 9 sps, 1 bl, 2 sps; rep from * across, end with 1 sp; ch 3, turn.

Row 12: Make 1 bl, * 11 sps, 2 bls; rep from * across, end with 1 bl; ch 4, turn.

Row 13: Make 91 sps; ch 4, turn.
Row 14: Make 91 sps; ch 3, turn.
Row 15: Rep Row 12.
Row 16: Rep Row 11; ch 4 (instead of ch 3), turn.
Row 17: Rep Row 10.
Row 18: Rep Row 9; ch 3 (instead of ch 4), turn.
Row 19: Rep Row 8; ch 4, turn.
Rows 20–24: Continuing in *reverse* order, rep rows 7–3.
Rows 25 and 26: Make 91 sps; ch 4, turn.

Rep rows 3–26 four times more. Fasten off.

■ For the weaving

PANEL 1: With burgundy and leaving a tail 6 inches long, crochet a chain 70 inches long. Thread one end of the chain into a yarn needle. Starting at the bottom of the background, weave the chain through the mesh across the long edge as described.

Row 1: Up in first sp, down in second sp, * up in next sp, down in next sp. Rep from * across to opposite end. *Note:* Be sure the chain goes under each block and that nubby side of chain is on *right* side throughout work.

Row 2: Make another 70-inch-long chain and weave through Row 2 of mesh as follows: Down in first sp, up in second sp, * down in next sp, up in next sp. Rep from * across to opposite end.

Rows 3–13: Make 11 more 70-inch-long chains and rep rows 1 and 2 of weaving 5 times more, then rep Row 1 once more.

PANELS 2–7: Make 78 chains; rep rows 1 and 2 of weaving 6 times, then rep Row 1 once more. Fasten chains to edges and weave in ends.

■ For the fringe

Cut 3 strands, each 10 inches long. Double these strands to form a lp. With *right* side of the piece facing you, insert hook from back to front through the corner mesh at the beginning of one end and draw lp through; draw loose ends through lp and pull up tightly to form a knot. Working across edge, make a fringe in each mesh sp. Trim ends evenly.

Candle Tree

Shown on page 104.
Finished size is 13¼ inches tall.

MATERIALS

15x28-inch piece of ⅛-inch-thick
   hardboard
Twelve ¾x¾x¾-inch pine blocks for
   candle holders
Wood glue
⁷⁄₁₆-inch drill bit
Jigsaw or band saw
Graphite or carbon paper
Twelve 6-inch-tall ½-inch-diameter
   candles
Latex primer
Green, red, and gold acrylic paints
Stencil brush
Paintbrushes
Sponge
Graph paper and pencil

INSTRUCTIONS

Enlarge the pattern, *right,* onto graph
paper. Transfer two trees to hardboard
with graphite or carbon paper. Cut out
the pieces with a jigsaw or band saw.

To make the intersecting slots, mark
the center of the tree at the halfway
point. Cut an ⅛-inch-wide slot into the
lower half of one tree and a corresponding slot into the upper half of the
second tree. Interlock the trees by slipping one slot into the other.

For the candle holders, drill holes ¼
inch deep into the pine blocks. Cut ⅛-
inch slots in the bottoms of the pine
blocks; glue and slide the blocks onto
the branch ends.

Prime the tree. Paint the tree green.
Sponge with gold paint. With circular
strokes of a stencil brush, dab red and
gold ornaments on the tree. Paint the
star gold and the candle holders red.
Insert the candles.

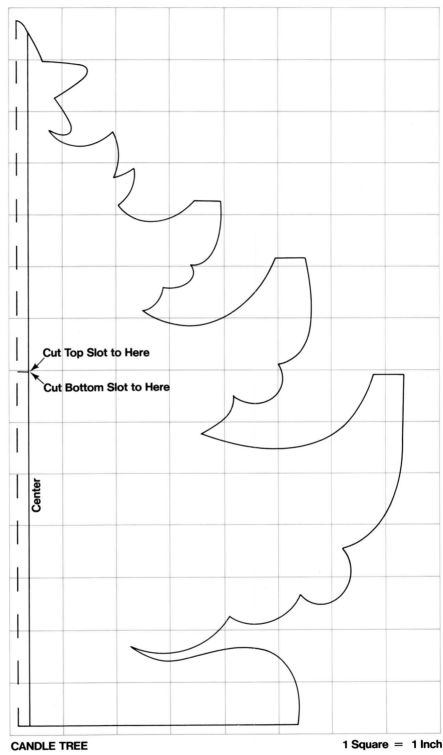

Cut Top Slot to Here

Cut Bottom Slot to Here

Center

CANDLE TREE

1 Square = 1 Inch

Christmas Cactus Appliqué Quilt

Shown on page 105.
Finished quilt is 84 inches square.
Finished block is 36 inches square.

MATERIALS

4 yards of muslin or white fabric
2¼ yards *each* of green, red, and gold fabrics
5 yards of backing fabric
Cardboard or plastic for templates
Quilt batting

INSTRUCTIONS

Trace and make templates for the patterns *opposite,* expanding the partial patterns along the fold lines into full patterns. Patterns A, D, and F and patterns C, E, and G are stacked as they will be in the finished block. Make a separate pattern for each piece. The patterns are finished size; add seam allowances when cutting the pieces. To use the templates for the appliqué shapes, trace around the templates on the *right* side of the fabric; cut out the pieces adding a generous ⅛ inch for seam allowances.

CUTTING THE BORDERS AND BLOCKS: Measurements for the muslin blocks, borders, and for the border corners include ¼-inch seam allowances. The borders are cut longer than is necessary; trim the borders to the length required after all the blocks are assembled.

From the muslin, cut four 36½-inch squares. Cut four 2½-inch squares for the border corners.

Cut four 2½x76-inch borders *each* from the green, red, and gold fabrics. Cut 2½-inch corner squares as follows: 12 squares *each* from the gold and green fabrics, and eight squares from the red fabric.

CUTTING APPLIQUÉ PIECES: From the green fabric, cut four A circles, 16 C pieces, 16 B swags, and 48 H teardrops.

From the red fabric, cut four D circles, 16 E ovals, and 48 H teardrops.

From the gold fabric, cut four F circles, 16 G ovals, and 48 H teardrops.

MAKING BLOCKS: Fold a large muslin square horizontally, vertically, and diagonally; crease to form placement guidelines for the appliqué.

Referring to the block design, *below left,* position the green A circle, B swags, and C ovals. Rolling under the seam allowances of each piece (see tip box on *page 112*), appliqué the pieces to the muslin. Leave the outside ends of the C ovals unstitched. Working from the *wrong* side, trim the muslin from behind the green pieces, leaving a scant ¼-inch seam allowance.

Position and appliqué red D circles and E ovals; trim green fabric from behind these pieces. Position and appliqué gold F circles and G ovals; trim red fabric from behind these pieces. Position three green H teardrops at the end of each C oval, slipping ends of the teardrops under the open end of the ovals. Position red and gold teardrops in the same way. Appliqué teardrops at the end of each oval.

Make four Christmas Cactus blocks.

ASSEMBLY: Sew the four completed blocks together; measure the quilt top. Cut all the borders to this length (approximately 72½ inches).

To make one border set, sew a green, red, and gold border together, with the red strip in the center. Make four border sets. Placing the green border next to the quilt, sew a border set to opposite sides of the quilt top.

Referring to corner block diagram, *opposite,* assemble small squares into four corner blocks. Positioning a gold square next to a green strip, sew corner blocks to ends of remaining borders. Sew borders to quilt.

FINISHING: Cut the backing fabric into two equal lengths. Cut one piece in half lengthwise. Matching selvages and taking ½-inch seams, sew one narrow panel to each side of the full panel.

Layer and baste the quilt top, batting, and quilt back. Quilt as desired.

When the quilting is complete, trim the batting ½ inch larger all around than the quilt top. Trim the quilt back 1¼ inches larger all around than the quilt top. Turn in ¼ inch on the quilt back. Bring the folded edge of the quilt back over to the quilt top, covering the raw edges; blindstitch in place.

APPLIQUÉ BLOCK DESIGN   **36-Inch Square**

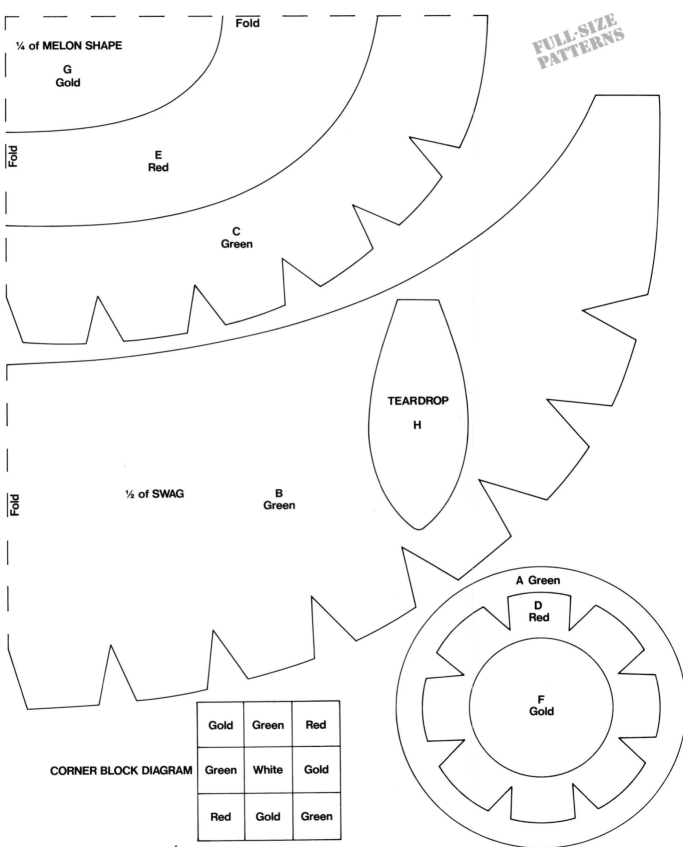

¼ of MELON SHAPE

G
Gold

Fold

Fold

E
Red

C
Green

TEARDROP

H

½ of SWAG

B
Green

A Green

D
Red

F
Gold

Fold

Gold	Green	Red
Green	White	Gold
Red	Gold	Green

CORNER BLOCK DIAGRAM

CHRISTMAS CACTUS APPLIQUÉ QUILT

Holiday Workshop

Tired of expensive, store-bought ornaments that all look alike? Make your tree unique by crafting your own carved ornaments. It's easy, even for inexperienced woodworkers!

Inspired by traditional Scandinavian motifs, ornaments cut from ¼-inch-thick basswood lend the warm tones of natural wood to a tree decorated in country style.

Leave the rocking horse, candle, tree, Eskimo, and snowman shapes natural, or paint them with water-thinned acrylic paints. Each ornament is 3 to 4¼ inches high.

Use a gouge or a V-tool for the carving. Using ¼-inch stock will provide enough thickness to carve deeply into the wood to create a dramatic relief effect. Select thinner stock if you prefer to wood-burn the details rather than carve the ornaments.

Choose a variety of acrylic paint colors to decorate portions of each carved ornament. When the paint is thinned with water, it makes a stain or wash that allows the beauty of the wood grain to show through.

Wooden Ornaments

Shown on pages 118 and 119.
Finished ornaments range from 3 to 4¼
inches high.

MATERIALS

One 4¼-inch-square piece of ¼-inch
  basswood for each ornament
Tracing paper
Graphite or carbon paper
Scroll saw or coping saw
Drill; ¼-inch and ¹⁄₁₆-inch drill bits
Bench knife (carving or whittling
  knife) to round off corners and
  shape carvings
½-inch shallow (No. 3 or No. 4)
  straight gouge
Approximately ⅛-inch-wide V-tool to
  carve outlines and details
Approximately ⅛-inch-wide small
  deep gouge for texturing
  ornaments
Green, red, gold, and brown acrylic
  craft paints
Boiled linseed oil
Small tube of raw umber artist's oil
  paint
Gold cord or thread for hangers
Woodburning tools (optional)

INSTRUCTIONS

Carve the ornaments with woodcarv-
ing tools, as shown in the photograph
on pages 118 and 119, or add the detail lines with woodburning tools.

Trace the full-size patterns, *right* and
opposite, onto tracing paper. Using
graphite or carbon paper, transfer the
outlines onto basswood squares.

Cut out the ornaments, using a scroll
saw or coping saw. To cut out the
openings on the candle and the hobbyhorse, drill a ¼-inch-diameter hole in
the area where the wood will be removed. Disconnect the saw blade and
thread the blade through the hole. Re-
connect the blade and cut out the
opening details.

Drill a ¹⁄₁₆-inch-diameter hole near
the top of each ornament for a hanger.

To create a rich, hand-carved appearance, lightly texture the surface of
each ornament with a ½-inch shallow
flat gouge. Using graphite or carbon
paper, transfer the design details onto
each ornament.

Leaving the back side completely
flat, slope or round off the outer edges
of the ornaments with a bench knife.
Referring to the photograph, round
off the candle, the Eskimo's face, and
other design details. Do not round off
the rocker on the hobbyhorse.

Recess the circular portion on the
candle ornament. Carve the tree
branches so they slope down from the
tree top and out from the center.

Using a ⅛-inch V-tool, outline all
the design details.

Using either the V-tool or a ⅛-inch-
deep gouge, feather the edges of the
Eskimo's parka and echo the circular
outline on the ring around the candle.

Using a bench knife, carve off all
saw marks from the outer edges of the
ornaments. Using the V-tool, sign and
date the ornaments on the back side.

Thin acrylic paints with water so that
their effect is like a colored stain on the
wood rather than a solid coat of paint.
Paint the ornaments as follows:

Using green paint, stain the tree, the
holly on the candle ornament, and the
snowman's scarf.

Use red paint to stain the hobbyhorse body, the heart, the tree stand,
and the snowman's hat. Add a faint red
blush to the Eskimo's cheeks.

Using gold paint, stain the ring
around the candle, the candle tip, and
the snowman's hair. Use the same
paint for the rocker, saddle, and eye on
the horse. Stain the mane and tail of
the hobbyhorse black.

Use brown paint to stain the tree
trunk, Eskimo's hair, and buttons on
the snowman.

Allow the paints to dry. To give the
ornaments a warm, antique appearance
and to preserve them, add a small
amount of raw umber paint to the linseed oil. Dip the ornaments in the
boiled linseed oil mixture or wipe the
ornaments with an oil-soaked cloth or
rag. Remove excess oil by wiping the
ornaments dry with a clean, dry cloth.

Allow two to three days for the oil
finish to completely dry. *Note:* Oil-
soaked rags are a potential fire hazard.
Properly dispose of oily rags immedi-
ately after use.

Hang the ornaments with gold cord.

WOODEN ORNAMENTS

FULL-SIZE PATTERNS

WOODEN ORNAMENTS

121

Christmas Stars and Snowflakes

Lacy snowflakes glistening on a frosty window signal that winter has come and Christmas is near. In crochet, cross-stitch, and appliqué, the star and snowflake motifs presented in this chapter make perfect holiday gifts and ornaments.

Four different appliquéd snowflakes lie like new-fallen snow on the gentle gray background of this 75x90-inch antique quilt, *opposite.*

One of these snowflakes is similar to one made by Charlotte Jane Whitehill, a renowned quilt maker of the 1930s, on a quilt now owned by the Denver Art Museum.

Full-size patterns and instructions begin on page 128.

Our collection of light and lovely snowflakes, *above,* includes both simple and intricate designs to crochet.

One ball of Size 30 crochet cotton and a Size 10 steel crochet hook are all you need to create a bounty of beautiful snowflakes. Each ornament is 4½ to 5¼ inches in diameter.

Trace and cut a flying bird ornament from a single sheet of white paper. Folding and gluing the wings

in place will quickly hatch an aviary of ornaments. Add a light dusting of silver glitter for an extra touch of sparkle, or create a flock of many colors by using different papers.

Add birds and snowflakes to a mobile of ornaments and greenery as shown, or use them as tree trimmers.

Cross-stitch lovers will be intrigued by the special stitches that

create unusual texture and dimension in this cross-stitch sampler, *opposite.* Easy to do, these stitches are completely diagramed on page 133. If you prefer, you can replace these stitches with regular cross-stitches.

Worked in folk-art shades of teal, taupe, and pink on 14-count red Aida cloth, the finished design is 8⅝x11¼ inches.

A complete stitching chart for the sampler is on pages 134 and 135.

Make an all-American Christmas with red, white, and blue ornaments. Our collection of flag-waving stars and snowflakes is ideal for those with a year-round patriotic spirit.

Quilters have used star patterns in countless ways, devising many variations on a few simple shapes. The five cross-stitched star motifs shown here are inspired by classic patchwork designs.

Crafted with four strands of floss, each stitch is worked over two squares of 14-count perforated paper. The finished ornaments are 4½ inches square.

Lovers of tatted lace will find an intriguing choice in the two snowflake designs. The small stars have five points; the medium and large stars have six points.

Work the small stars in the traditional tatting method using Size 8 pearl cotton and metallic thread.

The six-pointed designs are worked with an ingenious split-ring method in either Size 3 or Size 5 pearl cotton. Illustrated tips on this technique are on page 138. Gold beads sparkle at the tips of the smaller versions.

Instead of trimming a tree, use a garden-variety grapevine wreath and miniature flags to create a star-studded door or hallway greeting.

Snowflake Quilt

Shown on pages 122 and 123.
Finished quilt is approximately
75x90 inches.
Finished snowflake blocks are
15 inches square.

MATERIALS

7 yards of blue-gray fabric
4⅜ yards of white fabric
5½ yards of backing fabric
Quilt batting
Cardboard or plastic for templates
Nonpermanent fabric marker
Tracing paper and pencil

INSTRUCTIONS

TEMPLATES: Fold a 15½-inch square of tracing paper in half horizontally and vertically, dividing it into four quarters; make sharp creases along the folds. Align the folds with the dashed lines on one of the quarter patterns on pages 129 and 130. Trace the pattern onto *each* quadrant of the square. Make a complete pattern for each snowflake.

Trace around the separate elements of each snowflake design to make the appliqué patterns; use these tracings to make cardboard or plastic templates. Or, if you prefer, you can use a nonpermanent fabric marker to trace the elements directly onto the appliqué fabric. Do not cut the tracing pattern.

CUTTING: Measurements given for borders and the background squares include ¼-inch seam allowances.

From the gray fabric, cut two 8x94-inch side borders and two 8x79-inch top and bottom borders. From the remainder, cut twenty 15½-inch squares.

From the white fabric, cut two 2¼x94-inch strips for the side border trim and two 2¼x79-inch strips for the top and bottom border trim. From the remaining white fabric, cut twenty 15-inch squares for the snowflakes.

Lay out the templates for a snowflake design on the *right* side of one white fabric square. Use a light pencil or a nonpermanent marker to trace around the templates, leaving at least ¼ inch between each shape. Cut out all the snowflake pieces, adding approximately ⅛-inch seam allowances around each element. Cut enough pieces to make five snowflakes from each of the four designs.

APPLIQUÉ: Fold a gray square in half vertically, horizontally, and diagonally in both directions; lightly crease along the folds to create positioning guides for a snowflake. Unfold the fabric. Center and pin a snowflake on the background square. Use white thread to appliqué the snowflake onto the background square. See page 112 for tips on needle-rolling appliqué.

Make 20 snowflake blocks.

ASSEMBLY: Lay out the blocks in five horizontal rows with four blocks in each row, arranging the snowflakes in a pleasing manner. The quilt pictured on page 123 has the five flakes of each design running in diagonal lines from upper right to lower left.

Assemble the blocks for each row; join the rows.

ADDING BORDERS: To prepare the white strips for the top and bottom borders, bring the ends of each strip together to fold each strip in half. Referring to the border cutting diagram, *below*, snip out triangles along the length of the borders. The diagram shading indicates the areas that are cut away. When opened out, there will be 24 sawtooth peaks along the top of each border strip. Repeat for the white side borders, which have 30 sawtooth peaks along each border.

Position the sawtooth borders atop the corresponding gray border strips,

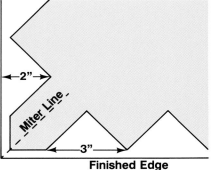

Finished Edge
BORDER CORNER DIAGRAM
SNOWFLAKE QUILT

aligning the straight bottom edge of the sawtooth strip with one edge of the wider gray border. Baste the two fabrics together along the bottom edge; appliqué sawtooth edge to gray fabric.

When the appliqué is complete, match the center of each border strip with the center of the corresponding side of the quilt top. Sew the borders onto the quilt top, mitering corners. The finished corners should resemble the corners sketched in the border corner diagram, *above*.

FINISHING: Cut the backing fabric into two 2¾-yard lengths. Piece the two panels together, using a ½-inch seam allowance. Trim seam allowance to ¼ inch, cutting away the selvage. Trim backing to 3 to 4 inches larger all around than the quilt top. Layer the backing, batting, and quilt top; baste the three layers together securely.

Quilt around the snowflake designs and around the block seam lines. Add additional quilting as desired.

To finish the edges, trim the batting and backing even with the quilt top. Fold under ¼ inch on both the quilt top and the backing. Hand-stitch the quilt top to the back, concealing the edge of the batting.

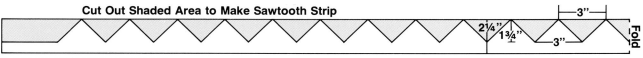

BORDER CUTTING DIAGRAM
SNOWFLAKE QUILT

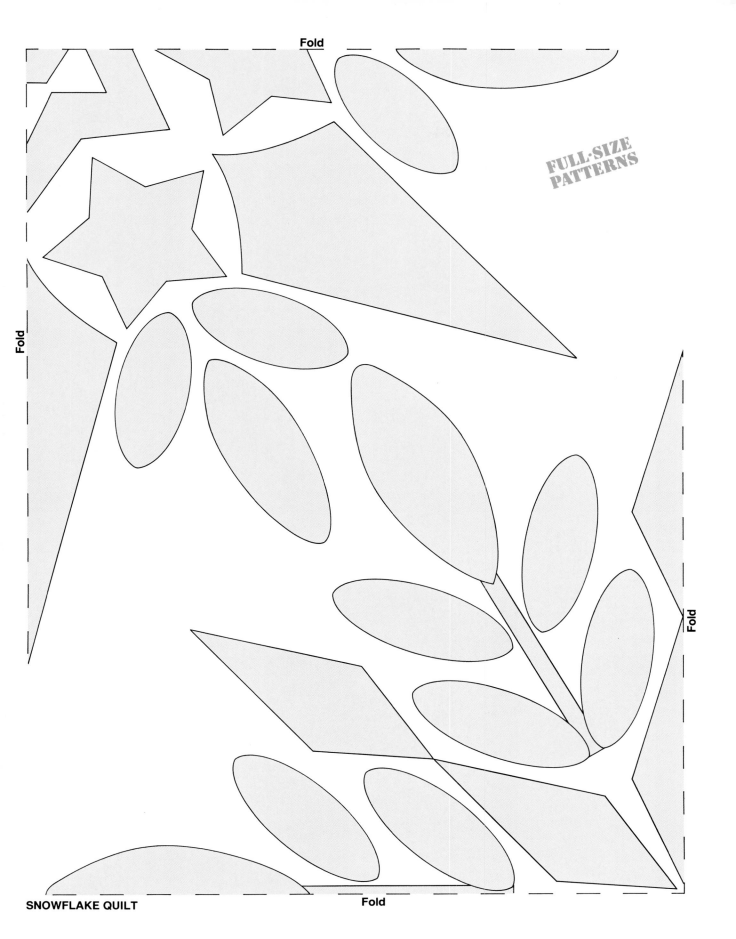

Fold

Fold

FULL-SIZE
PATTERNS

Fold

SNOWFLAKE QUILT

Fold

129

Stars and Snowflakes

Fold

Fold

SNOWFLAKE QUILT

Fold

Crocheted Snowflakes

Shown on pages 122 and 124.
Snowflakes are 4½ to 5¼ inches across.

MATERIALS
DMC Cébélia white crochet thread,
  Size 30
Size 10 steel crochet hook
Monofilament or thread for hanger
Glue or starch, cardboard, aluminum
  foil, and rustproof pins for
  stiffening (see page 132)

Abbreviations: See page 35.

INSTRUCTIONS
■ **Snowflake 1** (4½-inch diameter)
Ch 8; join with sl st to form ring.

Rnd 1: Ch 1, 18 sc in ring; join with
sl st to first sc.

Rnd 2: * Ch 12, sl st in fifth ch from
the hook; working a sl st in the first ch
of *each* of the next 10-ch lps, (ch 10, sl
st, ch 5, sl st) twice; ch 16, sl st; (ch 5, sl
st, ch 10, sl st) twice; ch 5, sl st; then sl
st in base of first ch-5 lp, sl st in the next
7 ch and in same st as beg ch-12 lp, ch
12, sl st in same st as last sl st; sl st in the
next 3 sc. Ch 12, sl st in the same st as
last sl st. Rep from * five times more.
Fasten off.

■ **Snowflake 2** (4½-inch diameter)
Ch 7; join with sl st to form ring.

Rnd 1: Ch 1, 12 sc in ring; join with
sl st to first sc.

Rnd 2: Ch 16, sl st in tenth ch from
hook and in next 6 ch, sc in same sc at
base of ch; sc in next st, ch 30, sl st in
23rd ch from hook; (ch 24, sl st in 21st
ch from hook) twice; sl st in next 2 ch;

ch 22, sl st in first ch at beg of ch
length; sl st in next 2 ch (of main stem);
ch 24, sl st in first ch at beg of ch
length; sl st in rem 6 ch to base of stem,
sc in same sc on ring, sc in next sc on
ring. Rep from * 5 times more; join to
first ch at beg of first stem; fasten off.

■ **Snowflake 3** (5¼-inch diameter)
Ch 8, join with sl st to form ring.

Rnd 1: Ch 1, 24 sc in ring; join to
first sc.

Rnd 2: Ch 5, (sk sc, dc in next sc, ch
2) 11 times; join to third ch of beginning ch-5.

Rnd 3: Ch 1, in *each* ch-2 lp around
work 3 sc; join to first sc.

Rnd 4: ** Ch 6, sk 2 sc, sc in next sc;
**ch 9, yo hook twice, draw up lp in
sixth ch from hook, (yo, draw
through 2 lps on hook) twice; * yo
hook twice, draw up lp in same ch,
rep bet ( )s twice; rep from * once
more; yo, draw through rem 4 lps
on hook—trc cluster (cl) made;** ch
6, sl st in base of cl, ch 3, sk 2 sc, sc in
next sc. Rep from ** 5 times more;
join last ch-3 to first ch of beg ch-6.

Rnd 5: Sl st in next 2 ch, * ch 12, **yo
hook 3 times, draw up lp in top of
trc-cl (yo, draw through 2 lps on
hook) 4 times—dtr made;** dtr in top
of trc-cl, ch 12, sc in next ch-6 lp. Rep
from * five times more; join last ch in
first ch of beg ch-12.

Rnd 6: * (Ch 8, sl st in third ch from
beg of ch) twice; ch 12, sl st in first ch,
(ch 6, sl st in first ch; sl st in base of
opposite ch-lp and in each of next 2 ch)
twice; sl st in same st as join, in each of
next 11 ch, and in dtr. Working a sl st
in second ch from beg of ch in *each* of
next ch-lps, ch 14, sl st; ch 10, sl st, ch
12, sl st; ch 10, sl st; ch 14, sl st; sl st in

base of first ch-14 lp, sl st in next ch, in
dtr, in next 12 ch, and in next sc; rep
from * around; end sl st in last 12 ch
and in same st as beg ch-8. Fasten off.

■ **Snowflake 4** (5-inch diameter)
Ch 6, join with sl st to form ring.

Rnd 1: Ch 4, work 11 trc in ring;
join with sl st to top of ch-4.

Rnd 2: Sc in sp bet ch-4 and next trc,
(ch 8, sk next 2 trc, sc in next sp) 6
times; join last ch-8 with sl st to first sc.

Rnd 3: Sl st in 4 ch; sc in same lp; (ch
12, sc in center of next ch-8 lp) 6 times;
join last ch-12 with sl st to first sc.

Rnd 4: In each ch-12 lp around work
14 sc; join to first sc.

Rnd 5: Sl st in next 7 sc, * ch 5, sl st
in next 4 sc; ch 18, sl st in first ch, ch
19, sl st in fifth ch from beg of ch-19;
ch 17, sl st in fifth chain from beg of ch-
17, ch 19, sl st in fifth ch from beg of
ch-19; ch 23, sl st in fifth ch from beg
of ch-23; sk next 6 sc, sl st in next sc; sl
st in next 3 sc; rep from * 5 times
more, ending sk next 3 sc and next 3 sl
sts, sl st in next sl st. Fasten off.

continued

Stiffening Snowflakes

After you've finished a crocheted snowflake or other crocheted ornament, you're usually left with a limp and shapeless piece of work. Take a few extra steps to turn your handiwork into beautiful ornaments you can display with pride. There are several ways to make crocheted snowflakes crisp and symmetrical. Here's a summary of the methods.

Clean the ornaments with warm soapy water, if necessary; rinse thoroughly. Press away excess moisture. Experiment with the methods outlined below on one ornament before completing a whole batch.

EQUIPMENT: In addition to the stiffening solutions explained here, some equipment is essential for perfect results.

Cotton threads, like most fabrics, will discolor unless you work with rustproof pins. Stainless steel straight pins, or other good-quality pins, are available at most notions counters. Larger T-pins, corsage pins, and florist's pins are easy to work with, too.

Use a piece of corrugated cardboard or foam-core board (available at art supply stores) to lay out the ornaments. Unless the board has a glazed or plastic finish, cover it with waxed paper or aluminum foil.

STARCH: Using liquid or spray starch to stiffen ornaments will enable you to launder them if they become soiled.

Follow the manufacturer's directions to prepare cooked starch for a very stiff finish.

Dip the ornament into the solution; press out excess starch between layers of paper towels.

Lay ornament on the working surface, and, beginning at the center, pin the ornament into a symmetrical shape. Pin each spoke of the snowflake straight out from the center; space evenly. Shape all the loops and picots to form a pleasing design.

To use spray starch, first dampen the ornament with water. Pin out the snowflake as directed above and saturate with spray starch. Let dry; repeat until ornament is stiff.

WHITE GLUE: Any household glue is suitable for creating permanent stiffening. Ornaments stiffened with glue can be cleaned with a damp rag or a soft brush.

To stiffen ornaments with glue, mix a solution of ⅔ glue and ⅓ water. Stir until liquids are thoroughly mixed. Dip the ornament into the solution and shape as for starch method described above.

ACRYLIC SPRAY AND DRAPING LIQUID: Clear acrylic spray (available at art supply stores) is a permanent stiffener that is easy to clean. Dampen the ornament; shape and pin to working surface. Allow to dry, then spray thoroughly. Repeat if necessary for sufficient stiffness.

Draping liquid, available at craft supply and fabric stores, is used to stabilize fabric-covered figurines and other projects. Follow manufacturer's instructions for application.

■ **Snowflake 5** (4¾-inch diameter)
Ch 10, join with sl st to form ring.

Rnd 1: Ch 4, ** trc in ring, ch 1, dtr in ring; ch 9, sl st in third ch from hook and in each of next 6 ch, sl st in dtr, ch 1, trc in ring, ch 1; * dc in ring, ch 1; rep from ** 5 times more, ending last rep at *; join last ch-1 to third ch of beg ch-4; fasten off.

Rnd 2: Join thread in any ch-3 lp at tip of any stem; * **ch 12, sl st in ninth ch from hook—first ch-8 lp made;** ch 1, trc in same ch-3 lp, ch 10, sl st in last trc; ch 1, trc in ch-3 lp, ch 12, sl st in last trc; ch 1, trc in ch-3 lp, ch 14, sl st in last trc; ch 1, trc in ch-3 lp, ch 12, sl st in last trc; ch 1, trc in ch-3 lp, ch 10, sl st in last trc; ch 1, trc in ch-3 lp, ch 8, sl st in last trc, ch 6, trc in ch-3 lp at tip of next stem; rep from * 5 times more; join last ch-6 with sl st to base of first ch-8 lp at beg of rnd; fasten off.

■ **Snowflake 6** (5¼-inch diameter)
Ch 8; join with sl st to form ring.

Rnd 1: Ch 3, 17 dc in ring; join with sl st to top of beg ch-3.

Rnd 2: Ch 1, sc in same st as join, * ch 8, sk 2 dc, sc in next dc. Rep from * 5 times more; join last ch-8 with sl st to first sc.

Rnd 3: In *each* ch-8 lp work 10 sc; join with sl st to first sc.

Rnd 4: * Working sl st in fifth ch from hook in *each* of following ch-9 lengths, ch 18, sl st; ch 16, sl st; ch 14, sl st; (ch 12, sl st) 3 times; ch 14, sl st; ch 16, sl st; ch 18, sl st; ch 3, sc in same st as join or last sc, (ch 7, sl st in fourth ch from hook) 5 times; ch 3, sk 9 sc, sc in next sc. Rep from * 5 times more. Join last ch-3 in same sc as beg ch-8. Fasten off.

FINISHING: To stiffen snowflakes, refer to the tip box, *opposite.* Form hanging loops with monofilament.

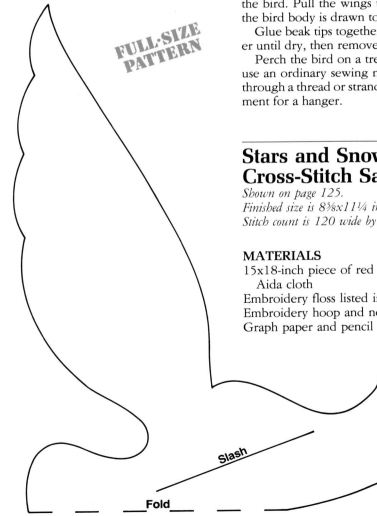

Paper Bird Ornament
Shown on page 124.

MATERIALS
Heavy white paper
Tracing paper and pencil
Scissors
Utility knife
Glue
Paper clips

INSTRUCTIONS
To make a full bird pattern, trace the half pattern, *below,* onto folded tracing paper and cut out. Use the tracing as a pattern to cut a bird from heavy paper. Use the utility knife to slit sides at slash line indicated on pattern.

To assemble the bird, slip the wing tips through slits from the underside of the bird. Pull the wings through until the bird body is drawn together.

Glue beak tips together; clip together until dry, then remove paper clips.

Perch the bird on a tree. If desired, use an ordinary sewing needle to pull through a thread or strand of monofilament for a hanger.

Stars and Snowflakes Cross-Stitch Sampler
Shown on page 125.
Finished size is 8⅜x11¼ inches.
Stitch count is 120 wide by 158 high.

MATERIALS
15x18-inch piece of red 14-count
  Aida cloth
Embroidery floss listed in color key
Embroidery hoop and needle
Graph paper and pencil

FULL-SIZE PATTERN

Slash

Fold

BIRD ORNAMENT

INSTRUCTIONS
Note: The shaded stitches on the chart on page 135 indicate where the pattern overlaps on page 134. *Do not repeat these stitches.* Read the complete instructions carefully before you begin to cross-stitch.

STITCHING: Begin working either at the center or at one corner of the design. Leave at least 3¼ inches of fabric on all sides of the design for mounting the finished sampler.

Use two strands to work the cross-stitches over one thread of Aida fabric.

First work all the cross-stitches and special stitches, then work backstitches. The basic cross-stitch, half cross-stitch, and backstitch are illustrated on page 157. Note that the points of the large stars are half cross-stitches.

SPECIAL STITCHES: *Note:* Both special stitches are worked with three strands of floss.

The star centers and the teal border are worked in the Smyrna Cross-Stitch. Shown in Figure 1, *below,* this stitch starts with a regular cross-stitch *worked over two threads;* it is completed by vertical and horizontal stitches that are also worked over two threads.

The stars in the lower design block of the sampler are worked in the Double Straight Cross-Stitch. Illustrated in Figure 2, *below,* this stitch starts with vertical and horizontal stitches *worked over four threads;* it is completed with a cross-stitch worked over two threads.

continued

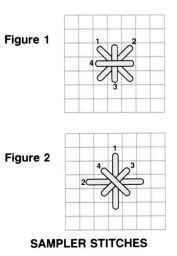

Figure 1

Figure 2

SAMPLER STITCHES

COLOR KEY

		DMC	ANCHOR
☐	Teal	924	0851
☒	Light Teal	926	0850
⊠	Taupe	642	0392
■	Light Taupe	644	0391
☐	Purple	552	0101
·	Pink	3689	049

STARS AND SNOWFLAKES SAMPLER

STITCHED BY

ABCDEFGHIJKLMNOPQRSTUVWXYZ

1990

1 Square = 1 Stitch

BACKSTITCH: All the backstitching is worked with one strand of floss. The backstitches on all the border snowflakes are worked with light taupe. The inner borders of the two design blocks are purple, as is the outline around the date. The personalization is worked in taupe; the date is worked in light teal.

For the personalization, work out the name to be stitched on graph paper, using the alphabet given. Leave one space between letters and three spaces between words, as shown in the words "Stitched By" on the graph. Match the center of your personalization with the center of the graph; work personalization in backstitches on the line shown.

FINISHING: Press stitchery on the back of the fabric. Frame as desired.

Perforated Paper Cross-Stitched Star Ornaments

Shown on pages 126 and 127.
Finished ornaments are approximately 4½x4½ inches.

MATERIALS

Sheets of white perforated paper
(Available at needlecraft shops or through Astor Place, Ltd., 239 Main Ave., Stirling, NJ 07980)
Embroidery floss in yellow, red, navy blue, and light blue
Tapestry needle
Monofilament thread

INSTRUCTIONS

Note: Perforated paper is fairly sturdy, so no frame or hoop is necessary for stitching. However, repeated ripping out and reworking of cross-stitches may cause the paper to tear.

Cut a 5-inch square of paper for each star. Trim around the star outline after stitching is completed.

Referring to the full-color charts for each star motif, *opposite,* use four strands of floss to work each cross-stitch over two squares of the paper.

When the stitching is complete, cut out the stars, allowing one square of paper beyond the stitching.

For the square ornaments, use four strands of floss to sew running stitches in a square around each star. (See stitch diagrams, page 157.) Work each running stitch over two squares and under two squares of the paper. Fill the square with a checkerboard pattern of yellow cross-stitches (see photograph on pages 126 and 127). Cut out the ornaments one square beyond the running-stitch edge.

Hang the ornaments using monofilament thread or tie them to a grapevine wreath with ribbon.

Six-Pointed Split-Ring Tatted Stars

Shown on pages 126 and 127.
Small star is 3 inches in diameter.
Large star is 4½ inches in diameter.
Recommended for experienced tatters.

MATERIALS

No. 3 white pearl cotton thread (large star)
No. 5 white pearl cotton thread (small star)
Two tatting shuttles
Crochet hook to fit thread if shuttle has no pick or hook
Six 5 mm gold beads for *each* star
White glue

Abbreviations: See page 139.

INSTRUCTIONS

Note: See the tip box on split-ring tatting on page 138 and the tatting abbreviations on page 139.

Wind 3½ yards of thread for a small star (6 yards for a large star) on one shuttle; wind 3 yards (or 5½ yards for large star) on second shuttle. Mark shuttles A and B.

If using beads on star tips, string six beads on thread of shuttle B. All picots should be ½ inch wide when open.

Metallic thread is not recommended for this pattern but can be used if tatting is done with a light tension. Do not use metallic thread on shuttle A.

Step 1: With A, work r of 3, (p, 2) twice, p, 3, clr, dnrw.

Step 2: With A, work r of 3, join to last p of previous r, (2, p) twice, 3, clr, dnrw.

Step 3: With A, work sr of 3, join to last p of previous r, 2, rs (color B), 5, clsr, dnrw.

Step 4: With A, work sr of 6, rs (color B), 5, p, 3, clsr, rw.

Step 5: Pull one bead from shuttle thread and position bet ring and little fingers of circle thread around left hand *before* tatting the first st of the following r: With B, work r of 3, join to p of last sr made, 3, push bead from circle thread close to last st made, 3, p, 3, clr, dnrw.

Step 6: With B, work sr of 3, join to last r made, 5, rs (color A), 6, clsr, rw.

Step 7: With A, work sr of 2, p, 3, rs (color B), 5, clsr, dnrw.

Step 8: With A, work r of 3, join to p of last sr made, 2, join to second previous r, 2, p, 3, clr, dnrw.

Step 9: Rep steps 2–8 four more times—5 of 6 points completed.

Step 10: With A, work r of 3, join to p of previous r, 2, join to middle p of first r made, 2, p, 3, clr, dnrw.

Step 11: Rep steps 3–6.

Step 12: With A, work sr of 2, join to first p of first r made, 3, rs (color B), 5, clsr. Tie and cut tails; dab knots with glue to keep them in place.

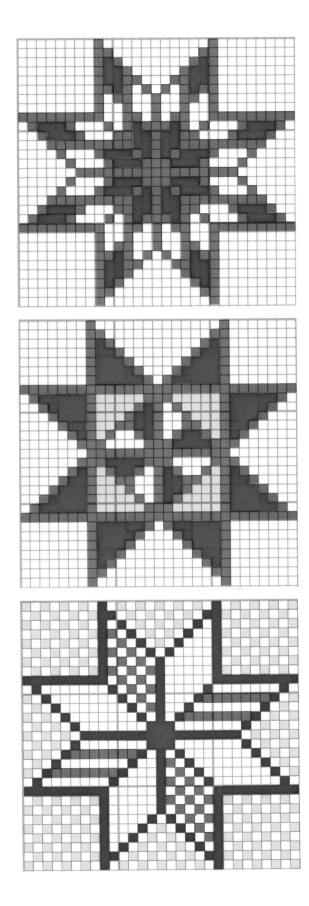

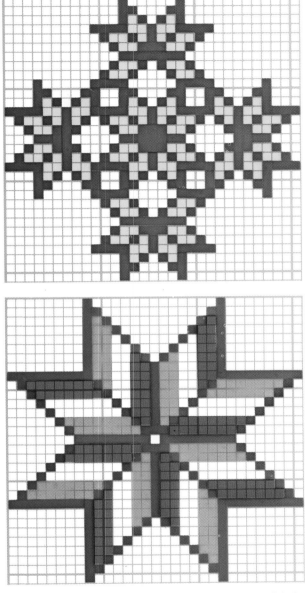

1 Square = 1 Cross-Stitch

COLOR KEY	DMC	ANCHOR
Red	666	046
Blue	797	0147
Light Blue	799	0130
Yellow	444	0291

CROSS-STITCHED PAPER STAR ORNAMENTS

Split-Ring Tatting

TATTING THE REVERSE
PART OF A SPLIT RING:
The reverse part of a split ring
is an upside down, backward
version of a regularly tatted
double stitch. Combined with
double stitches, it creates a
different-looking tatted ring.

Two shuttles (usually wound
with different thread colors)
are used for this technique.
Note: When practicing, it is
easier to learn the hand
manipulation if only one shuttle
is used and the second shuttle
is replaced with a ball of thread
of a different color.

Step 1: Position your hands,
shuttle, and thread as if
preparing to tat a regular chain.
Tie the beginning tails
together. See Diagram 1, *top
right.*

Step 2: Tat *wrong* stitches. To
do this, the fingers of the left
hand must *not* be relaxed at any
time while throwing the shuttle
or pulling on the shuttle thread
to form the stitch. The wrong
(or upside down) stitches
should be the color of the
thread on the shuttle, not the
color on the ball thread.

Note: If you pull the shuttle
toward your body to complete
the first half of the reverse
stitch (as you were taught *not*
to do when first learning to
tat), this will help prevent the
thread from "flipping" or
"popping" into a regular
double stitch.

TATTING A SPLIT RING:
Step 1: Mark shuttles A and B.
Leaving a 4-inch beginning tail,
use shuttle A to start a regular
tatted ring of 3, p, 3, do not

close ring. Take the circle
thread from the left hand and
turn it upside down; let shuttle
A dangle. See diagrams 2 and
3, *right.*

Step 2: Return circle thread
to hand with the beginning tail
hanging up and over the left
thumb, with the *first* stitch
between thumb and forefinger
of the left hand, and with
shuttle A dangling. Cross bars
of regular stitches and picots
should be facing down and to
the left or right. Circle thread
should be enlarged, but
comfortable, before you begin
the next step. See Diagram 3.

Step 3: Also grasp beginning
tail of shuttle B to reverse
stitch, beginning next to the
first stitch of the regularly
tatted stitches. Reverse stitch, 9.
See Diagram 4.

Remove circle thread from
hand. Pull on shuttle A thread
to close ring. **The only way
to close a split ring is by
pulling the thread from the
shuttle,** *not* **by pulling on
the beginning tail.** See
Diagram 5.

Diagram 6 shows several
practice rings in a row. Note
that the rings have picots on
the regularly tatted side; there
are no picots on the reverse
stitch side.

Step 4: Use the same pattern
as before to tat picots on the
regularly tatted side of the split
ring and put two picots on the
reverse stitch side, too. See
Diagram 7.

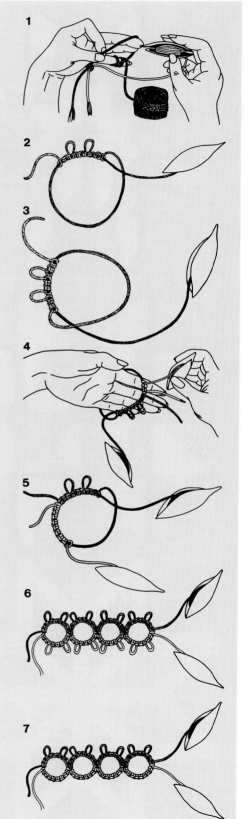

1

2

3

4

5

6

7

Tatted Five-Point Star Ornaments

Shown on pages 126 and 127.
Finished star is 2½ inches in diameter.
Recommended for experienced tatters.

MATERIALS
No. 8 white pearl cotton thread
DMC 2-ply gold metallic thread (size must be equal to No. 8 pearl cotton thread)
One ½-inch-diameter plastic ring for *each* star
Tatting shuttle
White glue

Abbreviations: See tip box, *below right.*

INSTRUCTIONS
Wind three yards of pearl cotton thread on shuttle. Use 1¾ yards of metallic thread from the ball.

All picots should be about ¼ inch wide when open. Use the diagrams, *right,* for tatting guide, working from top to bottom of each column.

Note: Use metallic thread for all chaining.

Step 1: Work r of 3, p, 3, join to plastic ring, 3, p, 3, clr, rw.

Step 2: Work ch of 8, rw.

Step 3: Work r of 3, join to last p of previous r (or to second previous r on each succeeding join after this one), 3, join to plastic ring, 3, p, 3, clr, rw.

Step 4: Work ch of 8, dnrw after and before each perimeter ring but *do* rw after each interior ring.

Step 5: Work r of 5, p, 5, clr, dnrw.

Step 6: Work ch of 8, rw.

Step 7: Rep steps 3 and 4.

Step 8: Rep steps 3–6.

Step 9: Rep steps 3 and 4.

Step 10: Rep steps 3–6.

Step 11: Rep steps 3 and 4.

Step 12: Rep steps 3–6.

Step 13: Rep steps 3 and 4.

Step 14: Work r of 3, join to p of second previous r, 3, join to center plastic ring, 3, join to first p of first r made, 3, clr, rw.

Step 15: Rep steps 4–6. Tie and cut tails; dab knots with glue.

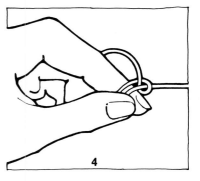

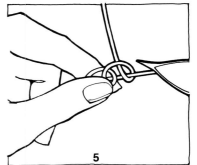

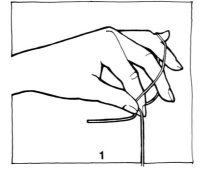

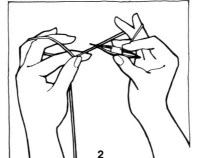

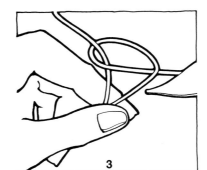

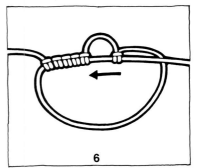

TATTING GUIDE

Tatting Abbreviations

ch	chain
clr	close ring
clsr	close split ring
dnrw	do not reverse work
p	picot
r	ring
rep	repeat
rs	reverse st

(Set first shuttle aside; remove circle thread from hand, turn it from top to bottom, then return it to left hand; add in shuttle B.)

rw	reverse work

(Turn work just completed upside down.)

sr	split ring

(If a direction step starts with sr, two shuttles will be used to make the next ring. If a step does not start with sr, you will be directed to do only a regular tatted ring with one shuttle.)

st	stitch

A
Victorian
Christmas

The age of Victoria is remembered
as a time of ornate elegance, of salons lavishly
filled with flowers, silk, and elaborate embroidery.
Recapture the rich Dickensian atmosphere of
those 19th-century holidays with crafts
inspired by old-fashioned lavender and lace.

Dried flowers make everlasting decorations that hold the fragrance of long ago. Rosebuds and greens glued into foam balls are the basis of the ribbon-hung pomanders, *left,* and the potted topiary, *opposite.*

Curtain lace adds a romantic edging to the bonnet and puffy-sleeved dress of this easy-to-sew 28-inch muslin doll, *opposite.*

Directions begin on page 146.

Needlework reached its apex with the doilies, counterpanes, and crazy quilts of Victorian times, when every well-bred young lady learned to ply needle and hook with great care and skill.

This crocheted table-cloth, *opposite,* is made of 110 squares of lacy pinwheels. Size 20 crochet cotton in a muted ecru color will resemble this 46x52-inch antique.

To achieve more of the patina of age, tea-dye the crocheted squares by immersing them in brewed tea.

Rarely has there been such intense interest in a needlework style as there was in Victorian crazy quilting. Women devoted themselves to embroidering randomly pieced fabrics into a riot of color and imagery.

The word "crazy" refers to the odd shape of the fabric patches used. These were "crazed"—irregularly broken up—in the same way as glaze for crazed china is cracked in an irregular pattern.

This crazy-patched holiday wreath, *above,* supports a personal collection of charms, buttons, and lace. An heirloom gift, you can add to it year after year.

Good fabric choices are velvets, satins, metallics, and ribbon. Patch them into a circle, then embroider the seams. Complete the 13½-inch wreath and decorate it with charms and other trims.

Like most immigrants, Josephine de la Croix came to this country with little more than she could carry. Leaving their farm in the French province of Alsace-Lorraine, her family set out for the American frontier.

The time was just after our Civil War, and the United States was once again a vibrant nation offering unparalleled freedom and opportunity. Joining the pioneers, Josephine and her husband made their way to Gallipolis, Ohio, in the 1860s.

The move forced the family to leave behind many valued possessions; only the most essential and precious things could make the journey. These were packed into a small chest made for the trip by Josephine's husband, Ameede de la Croix.

Among the treasures in that chest were five woolen coverlets on which Josephine had lovingly embroidered the varied flowers of her French homeland.

This dazzling red wool quilt, *opposite,* is one of the coverlets that came to America with Josephine de la Croix. Handed down through the generations, it now belongs to Josephine's great-great-grandson. The chest that carried it from France also remains in the family.

According to family records and traditions, Josephine was born on Christmas Day, 1831. In France, she made her living by doing needlework—handwork of fine lace and embroidery plus tailor-made clothing.

Her skill with a needle is evident in this lavishly embroidered quilt. Although the red is the same fabric all over the quilt, the fans are pieced from scraps of suiting and lining fabrics. The embroidery is a variety of stitches worked in lightweight crewel-type wool in a profusion of flora—each of the thirty-six 11-inch blocks is different.

The 71-inch-square quilt has seen many winters of hard use, showing a few stains and areas of wear. It remains in remarkably good condition, however, and now holds a place of honor among the heirlooms of Josephine's descendants. It is testimony to the talent of a woman who died long ago, but whose art lives on.

Full-size patterns and instructions to create your own version of Josephine's quilt begin on page 150.

Rosebud Pomander

Shown on page 140.
Finished pomander is approximately
4 inches in diameter.

MATERIALS

2-inch-diameter plastic-foam ball
3 yards of ½-inch-wide picot-edged
  ribbon
One piece of 20-gauge florist's wire
Approximately ½ pound of pink
  dried rosebuds and petals
Crafts glue
Clear acrylic spray sealer
Rose fragrance oil

INSTRUCTIONS

Spread the rosebuds out on paper. Select nicely colored buds with firmly attached stems. Save the loose leaves and discolored or damaged buds to create a potpourri mixture.

Spread crafts glue over the top of the ball. Beginning at the top center of the ball, push the stem of a rosebud into the ball. Add a circle of buds around it. As you add buds, direct the stems toward the center of the ball so they will not be in the way when you add successive rows of buds. Continue spreading the ball with glue and adding rings of buds until the ball is covered with buds. Remove one rosebud from the top of the pomander to make a place for the bow.

Set the pomander aside for one day to allow the glue to cure, then spray the pomander with clear acrylic sealer.

Using approximately 2 yards of the ribbon, make a bow. Secure the bow with florist's wire, leaving a 2-inch-long wire tail to secure the bow to the pomander. From the remaining ribbon, cut a strip for a hanging loop.

Place a dab of crafts glue on the ball where the bow will be. Push the bow wire halfway into the ball. Catch the ends of the hanging loop under the bow. Finish pushing the bow wire into the ball. Allow the glue to dry before lifting the pomander by its hanger.

Add a few drops of rose fragrance oil to the ball.

Victorian Doll

Shown on page 141.
Finished doll is approximately
28 inches tall.

MATERIALS

1 yard of unbleached muslin
1¼ yards of 12-inch-wide ring lace
  (sold for curtain valances)
2 yards of ¾-inch-wide picot edging
4 yards of ¼-inch-wide satin ribbon
1⅛ yards of 1-inch-wide satin ribbon
Doll needle
Natural quilting thread
Three ¼-inch-diameter shank buttons
Polyester fiberfill
Tracing paper and pencil

INSTRUCTIONS

Trace the full-size patterns on pages 147 and 148. *These patterns include ¼-inch seam allowances.* Cut all pieces for the doll and doll clothing from muslin. In addition, cut one 5x21-inch rectangle for the bonnet, one 13x36-inch rectangle for the skirt, and two 11x13-inch rectangles for the sleeves.

Note: Sew all pieces with right sides together, making ¼-inch seams and hems. Use quilting thread for gathers.

BODY: Stitch body front to body back, leaving openings between marks for the legs. Stitch pairs of arms and legs together, leaving openings at tops. Clip seam allowances on all five pieces; turn them right side out and stuff firmly with polyester fiberfill.

Using a doll needle and quilting thread, stitch legs into the openings along the lower trunk; sew openings closed. Fold seam allowance at top of arms to the inside; sew arms to body at circles on body pattern.

PANTALOONS: Stitch two pantaloon pieces together along the crotch seam; repeat for remaining two pieces. Stitch front to back at the side seams. Machine-stitch a narrow ¼-inch hem along the lower edge of each leg; topstitch picot lace edging to each hem. Stitch the inner leg seam.

Turn under a ¼-inch hem on the waist edge. Run a gathering stitch around the waist and around each leg, placing the leg stitch 1 inch from the

bottom hem. Fit the pantaloons on the doll. Pull gathers to fit the pantaloons to the doll at the waist and each leg; secure threads.

DRESS: Topstitch ribbon down the center of the bodice front, catching a row of picot lace under each side of the ribbon. Stitch the bodice backs together at center back from the bottom edge, stopping at the X indicated on pattern, *opposite.* Stitch bodice front to bodice back at the shoulders.

Make a narrow ¼-inch hem along one 13-inch-long sleeve edge. Topstitch picot lace edging over the hem. Starting 7 inches from the hemmed edge, stitch three rows of ⅛-inch-deep tucks, spaced ½ inch apart, parallel to the edge. Repeat for second sleeve.

Gather the top sleeve edges to fit the armhole curve of the bodice; sew sleeves to bodice. Stitch each sleeve and bodice side in a continuous seam.

Machine-stitch a narrow ¼-inch hem along one long side of the skirt piece. Starting 3 inches from the skirt hem (bottom), stitch three rows of ⅛-inch-deep tucks, spaced ¾ inch apart, parallel to the edge.

Cut a 36-inch-long piece of ring lace for the skirt bottom. Topstitch lace to the skirt bottom, inserting wide satin ribbon in the ring openings.

Stitch the skirt center back seam. Gather the top skirt edge to fit the bodice. Stitch skirt to bodice.

By hand, turn under and hem the neck edge of the dress.

Fit the dress on the doll. Turn under the seam allowances at the center back opening; stitch three evenly spaced shank buttons through both layers to close the opening.

Run a hand-gathering stitch around each sleeve 1 inch from the hemmed edge. Pull up the gathers to fit the arms snugly; secure threads.

Tie a length of narrow ribbon over the gathering stitching on sleeves and pantaloons.

Use the remaining lace motifs to embellish the dress. Place two small pieces of lace at each shoulder. Tie one large motif around the doll's waist with 14-inch-long ribbon ties sewn to each end of the lace.

continued

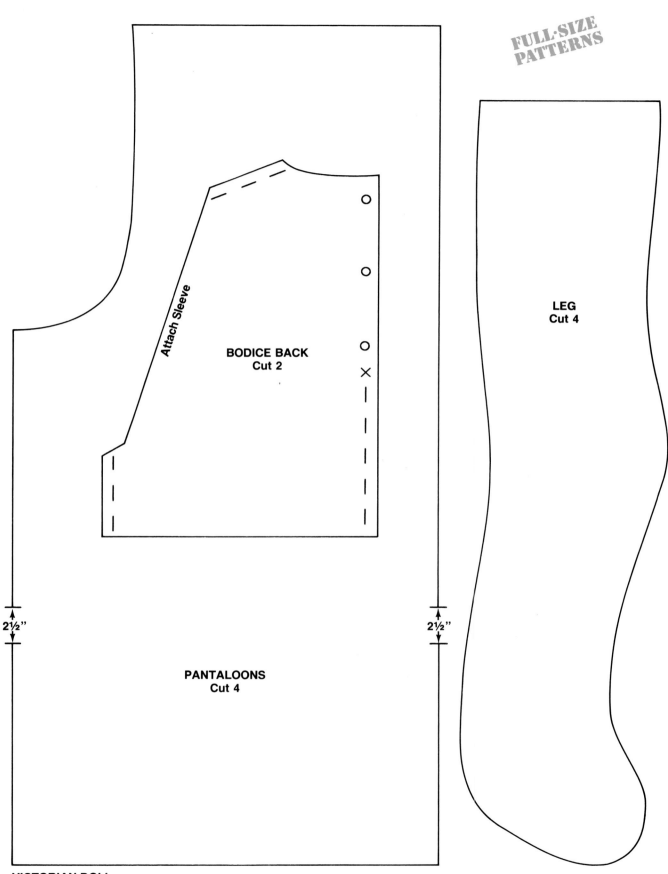

Attach Sleeve

O

O

O

×

BODICE BACK
Cut 2

LEG
Cut 4

2½"

2½"

PANTALOONS
Cut 4

VICTORIAN DOLL

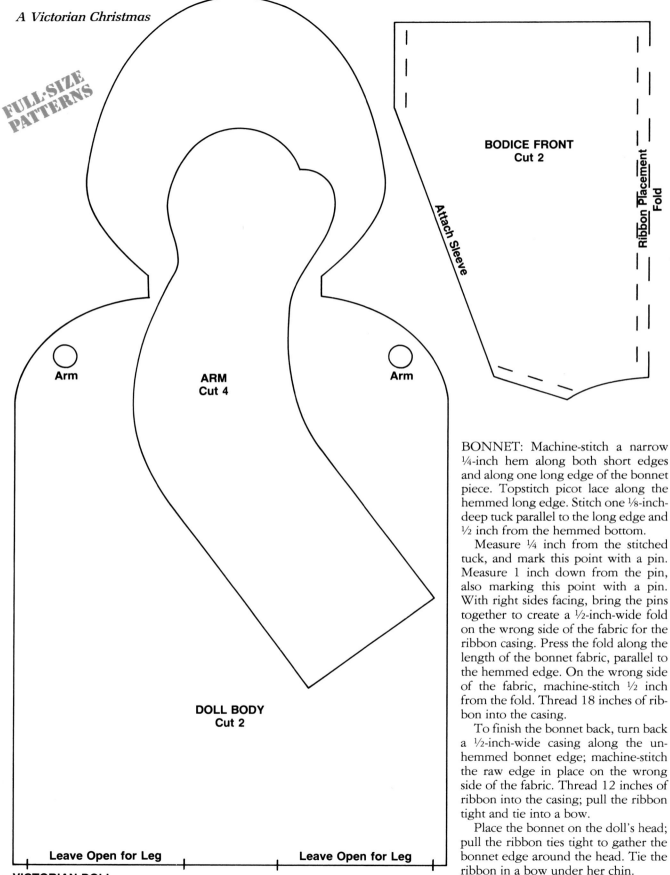

FULL-SIZE
PATTERNS

BODICE FRONT
Cut 2

Attach Sleeve

Ribbon Placement

Fold

Arm

ARM
Cut 4

Arm

DOLL BODY
Cut 2

Leave Open for Leg

Leave Open for Leg

VICTORIAN DOLL

BONNET: Machine-stitch a narrow ¼-inch hem along both short edges and along one long edge of the bonnet piece. Topstitch picot lace along the hemmed long edge. Stitch one ⅛-inch-deep tuck parallel to the long edge and ½ inch from the hemmed bottom.

Measure ¼ inch from the stitched tuck, and mark this point with a pin. Measure 1 inch down from the pin, also marking this point with a pin. With right sides facing, bring the pins together to create a ½-inch-wide fold on the wrong side of the fabric for the ribbon casing. Press the fold along the length of the bonnet fabric, parallel to the hemmed edge. On the wrong side of the fabric, machine-stitch ½ inch from the fold. Thread 18 inches of ribbon into the casing.

To finish the bonnet back, turn back a ½-inch-wide casing along the unhemmed bonnet edge; machine-stitch the raw edge in place on the wrong side of the fabric. Thread 12 inches of ribbon into the casing; pull the ribbon tight and tie into a bow.

Place the bonnet on the doll's head; pull the ribbon ties tight to gather the bonnet edge around the head. Tie the ribbon in a bow under her chin.

Dried Flower Topiary

Shown on page 141.
*Finished topiary is approximately
20 inches tall.*

MATERIALS
5-inch-diameter plastic-foam ball
6-inch-diameter clay pot
Small box of plaster of paris
Crafts glue
13-inch-long straight tree branch for
trunk of topiary
3 yards of 1½-inch-wide satin ribbon
Assorted dried greens, such as
boxwood, ambrosia, Sweet Annie,
and artemisia
Assorted dried flowers, such as
statice, roses, Queen Anne's lace,
lavender, perennial baby's-breath,
pearly everlasting, achilla, yarrow,
ageratum, globe amaranth, astilbe,
lamb's ear, thyme, and blue salvia
Dried moss
Florist's wire and green florist's tape
Optional: 18-inch-long grapevine

INSTRUCTIONS
If desired, wrap the optional vine
around the topiary trunk, securing the
vine at the top and the base with wire.

Mix the plaster of paris according to
package directions. Fill the clay pot
half full of plaster. Center the trunk,
pushing it into the plaster to bottom of
the pot. Add enough plaster around
the trunk to fill the pot to within 1 inch
of the rim. Let plaster dry.

Coat the top of the plaster with glue.
Cover plaster with moss and flowers.

Push the foam ball onto the top of
the trunk. Beginning at the base, cover
the ball evenly with greens. Add glue
to each stem before inserting it into the
foam ball. Trim greens to retain the
round shape.

Choose flowers with long stems. If
necessary, extend stems with florist's
wire and tape. Insert a variety of flower
textures and colors around the topiary,
adding glue to stems as for the greens.

Make a large ribbon bow, leaving
long streamers. Wrap florist's wire
around base of bow; insert wire ends
into foam ball to secure bow.

Pinwheel Tablecloth

Shown on page 142.
*Finished tablecloth is approximately
46x52 inches.*

MATERIALS
9 balls (400 yards) of ecru 3-cord
crochet cotton, Size 20
Size 9 steel crochet hook or size to
obtain gauge

Abbreviations: See page 35.
Gauge: Each motif is 4½ inches
square.

INSTRUCTIONS
Note: The cloth shown consists of 110
motifs. Work the first motif through
Rnd 11. Work all other motifs through
Rnd 10, then join to the previous motif
on Rnd 11. The assembled cloth consists of 10x11 motifs and a border.

When working into double crochet
(dc) of a previous rnd, always work
into the back lp.

FIRST MOTIF: Ch 6, join with sl st to
form ring.

Rnd 1: Ch 4; (dc, ch 1) in ring 15
times; join with sl st to third ch of beg
ch-4.

Rnd 2: Ch 3, dc in joining; * ch 4, sk
dc, 2 dc in next dc; rep from * around;
end ch 4, join with sl st to top of ch-3—
eight 2-dc grps.

Rnd 3: Sl st in next dc, ch 3, 2 dc in
next sp; * ch 5, sk dc, dc in next dc, 2
dc in next sp; rep from * around; end
ch 5, join with sl st to top of ch-3—
eight 3-dc grps.

Rnd 4: Sl st in next dc, ch 3, dc in
next dc, 2 dc in next sp; * ch 6, sk dc,
dc in next 2 dc, 2 dc in next sp; rep
from * around; end ch 6, join with sl st
to top of ch-3—eight 4-dc grps.

Rnd 5: Sl st in next dc, ch 3, dc in
next 2 dc, 2 dc in next sp; * ch 7, sk dc,
dc in next 3 dc, 2 dc in next sp; rep
from * around; end ch 7, join with sl st
to top of ch-3—eight 5-dc grps.

Rnd 6: Sl st in next dc, ch 3, dc in
next 3 dc, 2 dc in next sp; * ch 8, sk dc,
dc in next 4 dc, 2 dc in next sp; rep
from * around; end ch 8, join with sl st
to top of ch-3—eight 6-dc grps.

Rnd 7: Sl st in next dc, ch 3, dc in
next 4 dc, 2 dc in next sp; * ch 9, sk dc,
dc in next 5 dc, 2 dc in next sp; rep

from * around; end ch 9, join with sl st
to top of ch-3—eight 7-dc grps.

Rnd 8: Sl st in next dc, ch 3, dc in
next 5 dc, 2 dc in next sp; * ch 10, sk
dc, dc in next 6 dc, 2 dc in next sp; rep
from * around; end ch 10, join with sl
st in top of ch-3—eight 8-dc grps.

Rnd 9: Sl st across next 2 dc, ch 3, dc
in next 5 dc; * ch 10, sc in center of
next sp, ch 10, sk 2 dc, dc in next 6 dc,
ch 5, sc in center of next sp, ch 5; ** sk
2 dc, dc in next 6 dc; * rep from * 2
times more; rep once more from * to
**; end sl st to top of ch-3.

Rnd 10: Sl st across next 2 dc, ch 3,
dc in next 3 dc; * ch 5, 4 dc in next sp,
ch 10, sk next sc, 4 dc in next sp, ch 5,
sk 2 dc, dc in next 4 dc, ch 6, sc in next
sp, ch 1, sk sc, sc in next sp, ch 6; ** sk
2 dc, dc in next 4 dc; * rep from * two
times more; rep from * to ** once;
end sl st to top of ch-3.

Rnd 11: Sl st across next 2 dc, ch 3,
dc in next dc; * ch 5, 4 dc in next sp, ch
6, (4 dc, ch 10, 4 dc) in ch-10 sp—
corner made; ch 6, 4 dc in next sp, ch
6, sk 2 dc, dc in next 2 dc, ch 10, sc in
ch-1 sp bet 2 sc of previous rnd, ch 10,
** sk 2 dc, dc in next 2 dc; * rep from
* two times more; rep from * to **
once; end sl st to top of ch-3. Fasten off.

SECOND MOTIF: Work as for first
motif through Rnd 10; do not fasten
off.

Rnd 11 (Joining rnd): Sl st across
next 2 dc, ch 3, dc in next dc, ch 2, sl st
in corresponding sp of first motif, ch 2,
4 dc in next sp of second motif, ch 2, sl
st in next sp of first motif, ch 3, 4 dc in
next sp of second motif, ch 4, sl st in
corner sp of first motif, ch 5, 4 dc in
same sp of second motif (corner join
made). Work as for Rnd 11 of first
motif to complete, joining second motif to first motif at corresponding ch-sps
with sl st as established.

Make 108 more motifs, joining as
established into a rectangle of 10
blocks by 11 blocks.

BORDER: *Rnd 1:* Join thread in sp
before any corner. Sc in same sp; * ch
10, (sc, ch 10, sc) in corner; (ch 10, sc
in next sp) to next corner. Rep from *
around; end ch 10, join with sl st in
first sc.

continued

Rnd 2: Sl st across first 4 ch of next sp, ch 2, (sc, ch 1) three times in same sp, sc in same sp; * ch 7, **(dc, ch 2, dc)—V-stitch made** in corner sp, ch 7, [**sc, (ch 1, sc) four times—5-sc grp made** in next sp; ch 5, V-st in next sp, ch 5]; rep bet [ ] to within one sp of next corner **; work 5-sc grp in next sp, * rep from * twice more; rep from * to **; end sl st in first ch-1 sp of first 5-sc grp.

Rnd 3: Ch 2, (sc in next ch-1 sp, ch 1) twice, sc in next ch-1 sp; * ch 5, sc in sixth ch of next sp, ch 3, V-st in corner V-st, ch 3, sc in second ch of next sp, ch 5, [**(sc in ch-1 sp, ch 1, sk sc) three times, sc in ch-1 sp—4-sc grp made;** ch 5, V-st in next V-st, ch 5]; rep bet [ ]s to within last 5-sc grp before corner; ** 4-sc grp in next 5-sc grp; * rep from * twice more; rep from * to **; end sl st in first ch-1 sp of first 4-sc grp.

Rnd 4: Ch 2, sc in next ch-1 sp, ch 1, sc in next ch-1 sp; * ch 5, sc in next sc, ch 5, V-st in corner V-st, ch 5, sc in next sc, ch 5; [**(sc in ch-1 sp, sc, sk sc) twice, sc in ch-1 sp—3-sc grp made;** ch 5, V-st in next V-st, ch 5]; rep bet [ ]s to within last 4-sc grp before corner; ** 3-sc grp in next 4-sc grp, * rep from * twice more; rep from * to **; end sl st in first ch-1 sp of first 3-sc grp.

Rnd 5: Sc in center sc of 3-sc grp; * ch 5, sc in next sc, ch 5, in corner V-st work **(4 dc, ch 5, 4 dc)—shell made;** ch 5, sc in next sc, ch 5, [sc in center sc of 3-sc grp, ch 5, shell in next V-st, ch 5]; rep between [ ]s to within last 3-sc grp before corner; ** sc in center sc of 3-sc grp; * rep from * twice more; rep from * to **; join with sl st in first sc. Fasten off.

Crazy-Patched Charm Wreath

Shown on page 143.
Finished size is 13½ inches in diameter.

MATERIALS
16-inch square *each* of muslin for the wreath front and satin for the wreath back
Scraps of fancy fabrics, laces, and ribbons
Decorative buttons
Metal charms
Metallic threads
Scraps of embroidery floss
¼ yard of green moiré fabric for the bow
Beads; beading needle; and beading thread
2 yards of rattail cord
1 yard of 1-inch-wide ruffled lace for outer edge of wreath
Polyester fiberfill

INSTRUCTIONS
For the wreath pattern, draw a 14½-inch-diameter circle on paper; using pattern, cut out one circle *each* from muslin (wreath front) and satin (back). Cut a 4-inch-diameter hole from the center of each circle.

Assemble and pin a circular collage of fancy fabric shapes. Remove pins, and starting at the lower left corner with the first scrap right side up on the corner, attach the second scrap by laying it facedown over the first patch; sew the seam. Turn the material to the right side and press. Continue adding pieces in this manner until the circle is covered. Some seams will need to be sewn by hand in order to fit them in. If there are tiny gaps or raw edges left between blocks, you can appliqué a patch over them or later embroider a motif over them.

Hand-stitch laces and ribbons randomly over some seams; embroider the rest with feather or herringbone stitches. Refer to page 156 for embroidery stitches.

With right sides facing and using ½-inch seams, sew quilted circle to satin backing around the outside edge, leaving a 4-inch opening for stuffing. Stitch a ¼-inch seam around the inner circle, again leaving approximately 4 inches open for stuffing. Turn wreath right side out. Firmly stuff wreath with fiberfill through the openings; sew closed.

Add rattail cord around the perimeter of the center hole, sewing it down with a whipstitch. Around the outside perimeter, center lace widthwise over the outside seam; center the rattail cord on top of the lace and center seam, and whipstitch in place.

Randomly attach beads, charms, and buttons to the front of the wreath.

For the bow, cut a 6½x45-inch strip of moiré. Fold in half lengthwise, right sides together. Sew a ¼-inch seam along raw edges, leaving an opening for turning. Turn and press. Sew seam opening closed. Tie into bow, and tack onto the wreath. Add a charm to the center of the bow if desired.

Add a ribbon loop hanger to the back of the wreath, if desired.

Embroidered Fan Crazy Quilt

Shown on pages 144 and 145.
Finished quilt is approximately 71 inches square.
Finished fan blocks are 11 inches square.

MATERIALS
3 yards of dark red 60-inch-wide lightweight wool fabric (3¼ yards of 54-inch-wide fabric)
Scraps or ⅛-yard pieces totaling 2 yards of assorted fabrics (suiting, damasks, gabardines, tie silks, etc.) for fan petals
Thirty-six 5-inch squares of assorted fabrics for fan bases
4⅛ yards of 45-inch-wide cotton fabric or 2⅛ yards of sheeting for backing fabric
Lightweight yarns (crewel or baby weights) for embroidery in assorted colors, such as green, red, pink, yellow, cream, and gold
Cardboard or plastic for templates
Nonpermanent fabric marker
Tracing paper and pencil

INSTRUCTIONS
Note: See page 156 for embroidery stitch diagrams. Floral embroidery designs from the quilt on pages 144–145 are on the following four pages.

CUTTING: From the red wool fabric, cut two strips 3x67 inches and two strips 3x72 inches. Set these aside for borders. From the remaining wool fabric, cut thirty-six 11½-inch squares.

Make templates for bases and petals using patterns, *opposite.* From assorted fabrics, cut 36 bases and 252 petals, adding a ¼-inch seam allowance on all sides of the templates.

FAN BLOCKS: Piece seven petals into one fan, alternating petal colors. Press seams to one side.

Leave seam allowances flat at sides and bottom of fan; turn under ¼-inch seam allowance at top edge and press.

Turn under the seam allowance on the curved edge of the fan base. Baste fan base to bottom of fan, aligning straight edges at sides.

With yarn, work seven spokes of featherstitches in one color on fan base as illustrated. Use another color of yarn for featherstitching over each fan seam line.

Baste fan onto red wool square, aligning straight edges at sides. Work featherstitch along curved edge of fan, using the feathering to appliqué the fan onto the base square. Trim base square away under the fan, leaving a ¼-inch seam allowance at the curved edge of the fan.

Make 36 fan blocks.

ASSEMBLY: Work embroidery as desired on wool fabric, working the designs around the curve of the fan.

Lay out the finished blocks in six rows of six blocks each, turning the fans in different ways to achieve a pleasing arrangement. Sew blocks together in horizontal rows, using a ¼-inch seam allowance. Assemble the rows, matching the block seam lines carefully.

Sew the shorter border strips to opposite sides of the quilt top. Trim even with quilt. Sew long border strips to remaining sides; trim excess fabric.

Work embroidery around the border, curving the vine motif around the corner as illustrated on page 153.

BACKING: Because Victorian crazy quilts were usually intended for show rather than practical use, they differ from "real" quilts in that they do not include an inner layer of batting, or filling. The embroidered top was simply sewn to a backing around the edges, with no quilting or tying at the center; you can tie it to the top at block corners if you prefer.

Assemble backing fabric into a 72-inch square. Lay backing on top of quilt, right sides together. Sew around all edges, pivoting at corners, using a ½-inch seam allowance; leave an opening in one side for turning.

Turn quilt right side out through opening. Use a thin, blunt tool to push out nice sharp corners. Press with cool iron. Sew opening closed by hand.

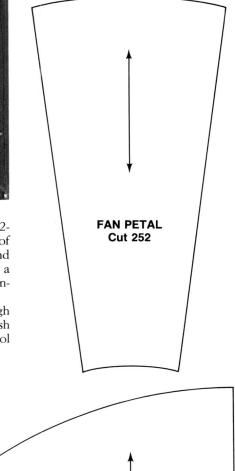

FAN PETAL
Cut 252

FULL-SIZE PATTERNS

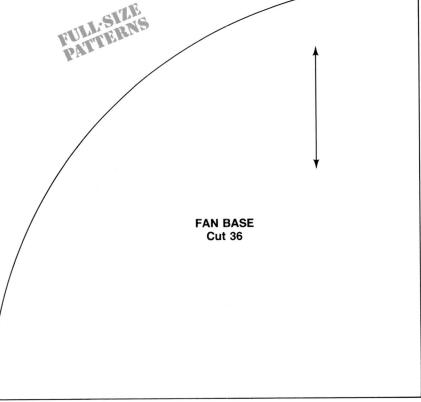

FAN BASE
Cut 36

EMBROIDERED FAN CRAZY QUILT

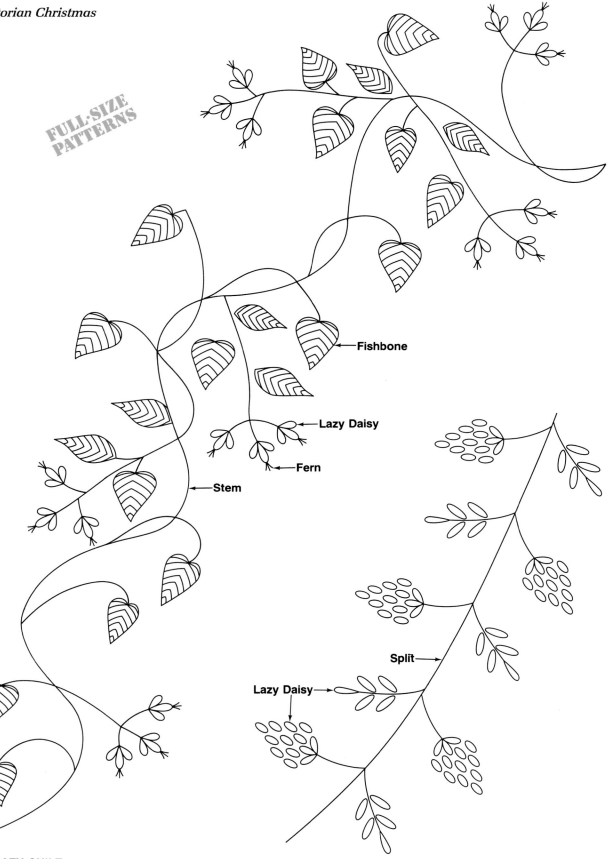

FULL-SIZE PATTERNS

Fishbone

Lazy Daisy

Fern

Stem

Split

Lazy Daisy

FAN CRAZY QUILT

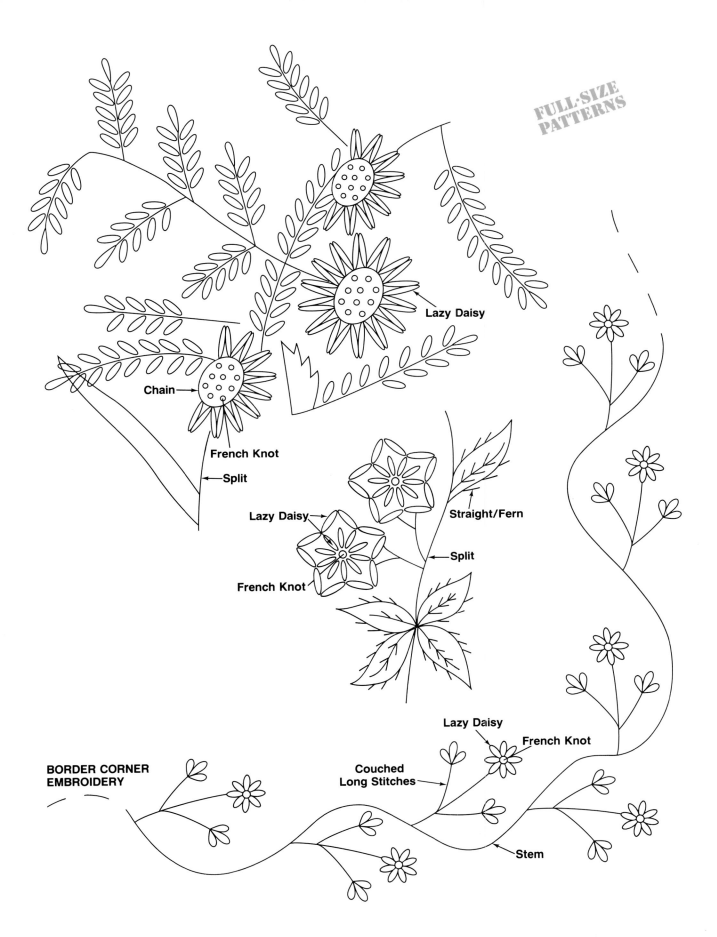

FULL-SIZE PATTERNS

Lazy Daisy

Chain

French Knot

Split

Lazy Daisy

French Knot

Straight/Fern

Split

Lazy Daisy

French Knot

Couched Long Stitches

Stem

BORDER CORNER EMBROIDERY

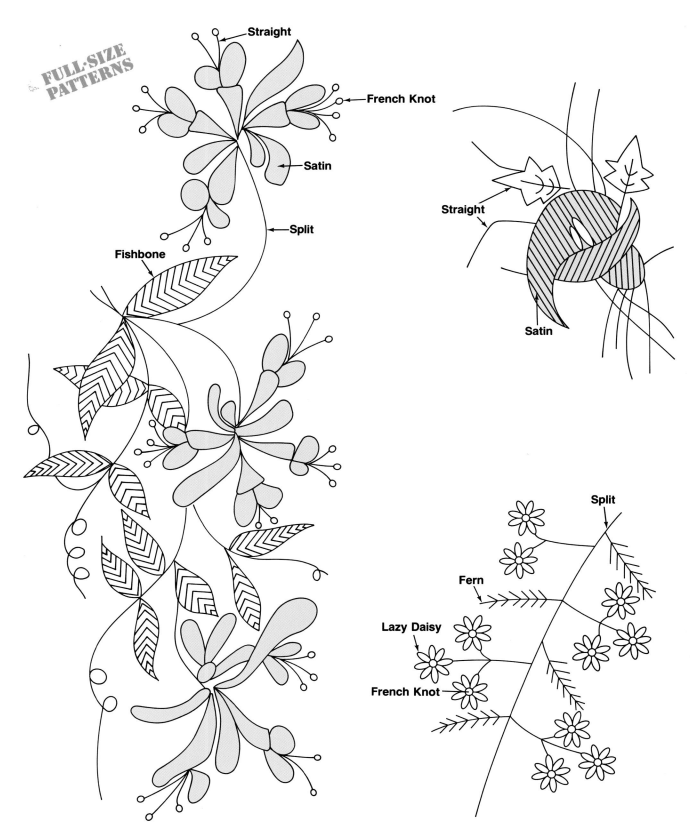

FULL-SIZE PATTERNS

Straight

French Knot

Satin

Split

Fishbone

Straight

Satin

Split

Fern

Lazy Daisy

French Knot

FAN CRAZY QUILT

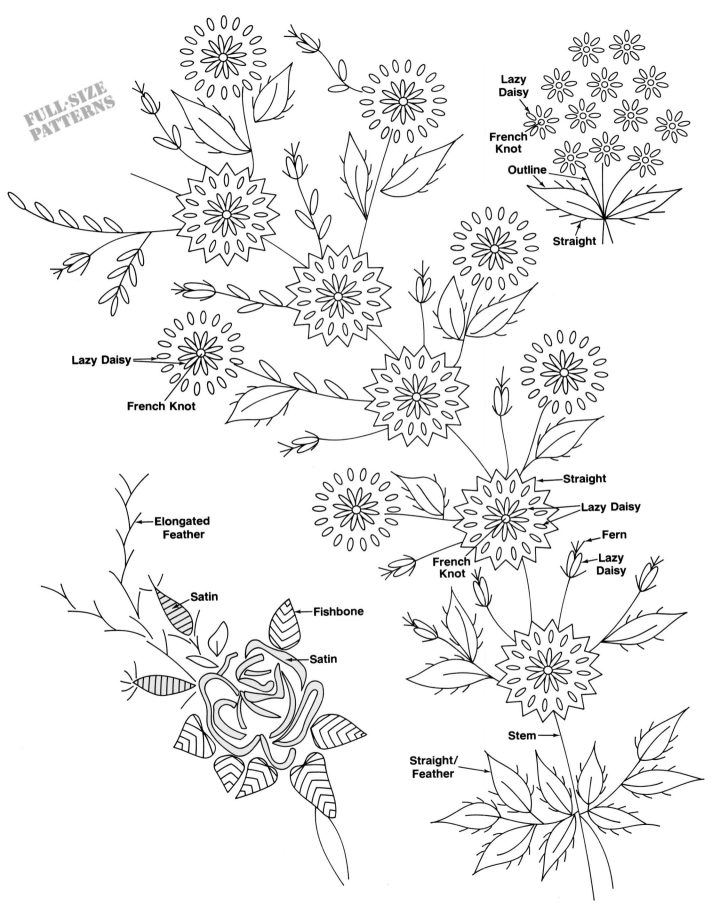

FULL-SIZE PATTERNS

Lazy Daisy

French Knot

Outline

Straight

Lazy Daisy

French Knot

Elongated Feather

Satin

Fishbone

Satin

Straight

Lazy Daisy

Fern

Lazy Daisy

French Knot

Stem

Straight/ Feather

Basic Embroidery Stitches

Use these embroidery stitch diagrams as a guide to create the
designs on the Embroidered Fan Crazy Quilt and other projects.

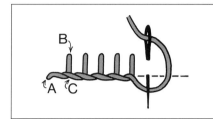

BUTTONHOLE STITCH

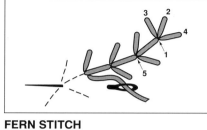

FERN STITCH

OUTLINE (or STEM) STITCH

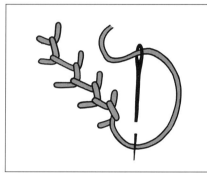

FEATHERSTITCH

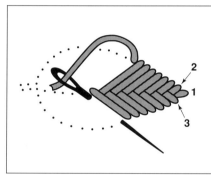

FISHBONE STITCH

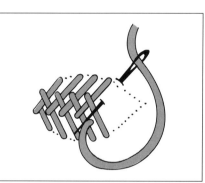

OPEN FISHBONE STITCH

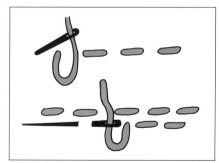

RUNNING (or DARNING) STITCH

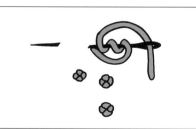

FRENCH KNOT

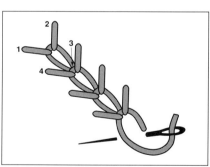

WHEATEAR STITCH

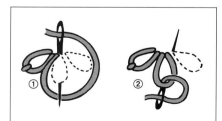

LAZY DAISY STITCH

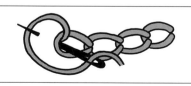

CHAIN STITCH

COUCHING STITCH

Basic Needlepoint and Cross-Stitches

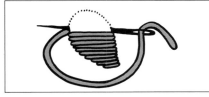

SEED STITCH

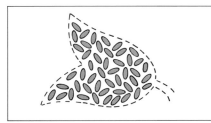

SATIN STITCH

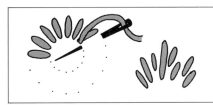

STRAIGHT STITCH

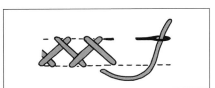

HERRINGBONE STITCH

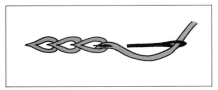

SPLIT STITCH

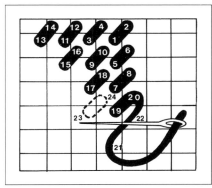

BASKET-WEAVE STITCH

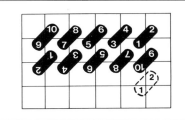

CONTINENTAL STITCH

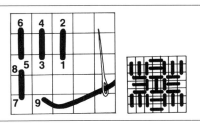

UPRIGHT GOBELIN STITCH

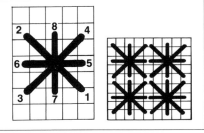

SMYRNA STITCH

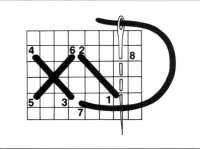

CROSS-STITCH

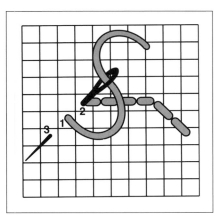

HALF CROSS-STITCH

BACKSTITCH

CREDITS

We would like to express our gratitude and appreciation to the many people who helped with this book.

Our heartfelt thanks go to each of the artists and designers, who so enthusiastically contributed ideas, designs, and projects.

Thanks also to the photographers, whose creative talents and technical skills added much to the book.

We are happy as well to acknowledge our indebtedness to the companies, collectors, crafters, and others who generously shared their stitched pieces and projects with us, or who in some other way contributed to the production of this book.

Designers

Appalachian Crafts—89, corn-husk angels
Aster Place Herbs—140, pomanders
Linda Beardsley—44, teapot pillow
Tess Boernke—10, toy soldier doll
Mary Sue Bruce-Kuhn—126–127, tatting
Susan Carson—66; 67, table
Coats and Clark—102
Laura Collins—126–127, cross-stitch
Sue Cornelison—125
Phyllis Dunstan—6–7, sugarplum bears; 8, moonbeam ornament; 45, grandparent dolls
Pam Dyer—98–99
Kathy Engel—10, ballerina doll; 100
Sandi Guely—24, stocking doll
Heritage Imports—141, doll
Jamie Hughet—24, stocking bear
Lynette Jensen—80–81

Becky Jerdee—104
Gail Kinkead—24, crocheted lamb; 64–65, crocheted hearts
Nancy Kluender—26, sampler
Margaret Leonardo—88
Pat Lose—84–85, angels; 86; 87, angels
Jude Martin—25
Genevieve Mason—122, ornament; 124
Judith Montano—143
Kathy Moore—45, strawberry ornament
Sandi Moran—64–65, wax hearts
Mary Ann Patrick—68, sweater
Joan Pratt—141, topiary
Nancy Reames—60–61
Harley Refsal—118–119
Beverly Rivers—87, stars
Saran Robinson—64–65, scherenschnitte
Valerie Root—48; 101
Helene Rush—46, 47
Sharon Ryback—38–39
Renée Schwarz and André Duchastel—26–27
Jilann Severson—67, snowball garland and starburst ornament
Barb Smith—68, snowbaby doll; 84–85, star ornament
Jane Swanson—69
Sara Jane Treinen—6, cone ornament
Julie Blashy Van Horn—89, plaque
Jim Williams—6, gumdrop garland; 8, peppermint garland; 43; 66, sampler
Dee Witmack—9, candy wreath; 11

Photographers

Dennis Becker—140
Hopkins Associates—24–25; 38–39; 46–47; 69; 84–85; 88; 126–127; 194
Michael Jensen—105
Scott Little—26–27; 49; 64–65; 86; 100; 122–123
William Stites—42–45
Perry Struse—cover; 3; 6–11; 66–68; 80–81; 87; 89; 98–99; 101–103; 118–119; 122; 124–125; 140–142; 144–145

Acknowledgments

Bartlettyarns, Inc.
Dept. BH
Harmony, ME 04942

Bates Anchor, Inc.
212 Middlesex Ave.
Chester, CT 06412

Buckboard Antiques and Quilts
Judy Howard
1411 N. May
Oklahoma City, OK 73107

Coats and Clark, Inc.
Dept. CS
P.O. Box 1010
Toccoa, GA 30577

DMC Corporation
197 Trumbull St.
Elizabeth, NJ 07206

Paul Ecke Poinsettia Ranch
P.O. Box 488
Encinatas, CA 92024

Mr. and Mrs. Vaughn Gayman

Harrisville Designs
Harrisville, NH 03450

Heritage Imports
P.O. Box 328
Pella, IA 50219

Madison County Historical Society
Winterset, Iowa

Marti and Dick Michell

Frances Rubin

Martin Schmidt & Sons
262 NW. Miller Road
Portland, OR 97229

Tahki Imports, Ltd.
11 Graphic Place
Moonachie, NJ 07074

INDEX

Page numbers in **bold** type indicate photographs; other page numbers indicate how-to instructions and patterns.

Have BETTER HOMES AND GARDENS® magazine delivered to your door. For information, write to:
ROBERT AUSTIN
P.O. BOX 4536
DES MOINES, IA 50336